CHOOSING
☆ THE ☆
PRESIDENT

1984

CHOOSING
☆ THE ☆
PRESIDENT

1984

by
**The League of Women Voters
Education Fund**

NICK LYONS BOOKS
SCHOCKEN BOOKS
New York

Copyright ©1984 by The League of Women Voters Education Fund

All rights reserved
Published by Schocken Books, 1984
Produced by:
Nick Lyons Books
212 Fifth Avenue
New York, NY 10010

Manufactured in the United States of America
ISBN: 0-8052-0763-5

For additional information on topics discussed in this book write to:
The League of Women Voters Education Fund
1730 M Street, NW
Washington, DC 20036

Library of Congress Cataloging in Publication Data
Main entry under title:

Choosing the president, 1984.

　　1. Presidents—United States—Election—1984
I. League of Women Voters (U.S.). Education Fund.
JK526 1984　　　324.973'0927　　　83-40462

CONTENTS

*"Governments are instituted among men,
deriving their just powers from the consent of the governed."*

The force behind these words is as powerful today as it was on July 4, 1776, when colonial patriot John Hancock and others signed their names to the Declaration of Independence.

The government of the United States continues to derive its powers from the people of this great nation. We are reminded of this truth every four years when we elect a president—just as we should be mindful at every election for a mayor, a town school committee member or a county official.

The John Hancock companies are honored to underwrite the 1984 edition of *Choosing the President*. We join with the League of Women Voters Education Fund in encouraging you to become involved in the political process and to play your role in choosing the president in 1984.

John Hancock Mutual Life Insurance Company

ACKNOWLEDGMENTS

To give due credit to others in the making of a book is always a difficult task. It is particularly true in the case of *Choosing the President,* which has been published and republished for some time now in editions tied to presidential election years. This edition builds on the work of many over the past decade. The 1972 edition was principally the work of Mary Morgan, with the help of Daphne White. The research and major revisions in the 1976 edition were the work of Annette Kornblum, under the supervision of Beth Perkins, with rewriting done by Madelyn A. Bonsignore. The revisions for the 1980 edition were made by Sheri Lanoff, with the help of Karen Lebovich.

Major revisions for the 1984 edition were made to reflect new information on voting behavior, campaign finance and delegate selection, and to update the entire manuscript as well. The 1984 revisions are the work of Mary N. Stone, Marlene Cohn and Patricia M. Hawkins, assisted by Marie Tessier and Matthew Freeman, under the supervision of Mary Stone. They wish to acknowledge with particular gratitude the help of Joseph Gorman and Joseph Cantor of the Congressional Research Service, Louise Lindblom of the staff of the Democratic National Committee and Catherine E. Gensior of the staff of the Republican National Committee.

The League of Women Voters Education Fund is especially grateful to the John Hancock Mutual Life Insurance Company for financial support for the 1984 edition of *Choosing the President.*

☆ 1 ☆

ON CHOOSING THE PRESIDENT

The president of the United States is probably the most important elected official in the world. The United States Constitution, political realities and historical precedents combine to give the president a position in the American system of government unmatched by that of executives in other democratic countries. Indeed, even executives in nondemocratic countries may not be as strong. They must give considerable attention to the possibility of overthrow, whereas presidents of the United States rest secure in the knowledge that their power is based upon consent.

Over the years, the powers of the president as outlined in the Constitution have been greatly expanded by many occupants of the office. The president has emerged as the chief political figure in the United States, despite the checks and balances established by the separation of powers and the federal system of government. With an election system that makes the executive branch politically independent of the other two branches of government and gives presidents *de facto* leadership of their political parties, our chief executives have usually won their battles with Congress and with the Supreme Court. Recent presidents have been aided by their large and expert staffs. Although power ebbs and flows among the three branches of government, the modern president plays a pivotal role in the whole structure.

9

Twentieth-century demands on government have further encouraged this trend. The president commands the large military forces of the nation and the major part of a vast civil bureaucracy. In addition, we expect the president to develop and push for legislation in areas of national concern, to serve as a symbol of the nation united and even to establish and maintain trends in national morals and mores. Historically the key figure in American foreign policy, the president, particularly over the past 45 years, has had increasing influence in domestic policy as well. Whether negotiating a disarmament treaty, instituting wage controls, talking to astronauts or formulating a major tax policy, the president clearly affects the life of every person in America. The choosing of a president, then, is of great significance to every American.

Television broadcasts of national party conventions and candidate debates draw millions of people into the excitement of nominating and electing the president and vice-president. Some watch these proceedings only as spectators. Others feel the personal involvement that comes from understanding and participating in the process.

Only if one knows how political parties function and how they fit into the governmental structure can one understand fully how a presidential candidate becomes a party's official nominee. It helps to know a few details about how the national political party conventions are organized and how they operate. In this multimedia age it is also important to be aware of campaign techniques, strategies and costs. The Federal Election Campaign Act (FECA) of 1971 as amended has made significant changes in the funding of federal elections. Finally, the expansion of the franchise over the last 20 years suggests an even greater need to understand all phases of the election process, so that individuals can more clearly perceive how to be effective—how to have their voices heard in the choosing of the president.

A president is elected only once every four years, but the *process* of election never really stops; it simply moves from one phase to the next. The preliminaries extend over roughly three years—from the presidential inauguration on January 20 to January 1 of the next presidential election year.

This is the time for a future presidential contender to build a strong and far-reaching record (either as an officeholder or as a spokesperson for a broad national constituency), to gain the attention of the media, to develop solid areas of political strength and to secure political commitments and endorsements.

The first great painting of an American political scene was depicted by John Lewis Krimmel. It shows an election day at the State House in Philadelphia in 1815.

The next phase begins with the election year and extends to the national conventions. Contenders must now decide whether to become candidates and, if so, in which states to concentrate their efforts. Delegates to the national conventions are selected during this period through either party caucuses or primaries, and candidates attempt to gain support from as many states as possible.

The next stage covers the week or so that each national convention is in session. This can be a time of high drama as candidates for president and vice-president are finally nominated and party platforms are nailed down. Losing contenders at the convention may close ranks behind the winner, choose to sit out the election or secede from their party and lead third-party or independent movements of their own. Next comes the presidential campaign, extending from summer to election day in

November. The final phase encompasses the election itself, the formalization of the results and the inauguration.

The presidential election takes place within the context of a well-established political framework: a system of institutionalized political parties and a large and ever-changing electorate. Most presidential candidates are nominated by political parties, campaign as partisans and are assisted to election by parties.

At every stage in the election process the voters are called upon to make choices. They assess the records of the various contenders, often express a preference in a precinct caucus or a primary, evaluate the convention choices and vote on election day. Many citizens will also campaign on behalf of their candidate in primary and election campaigns.

Choosing the President describes the political framework for presidential elections: first the political parties, then the voters; the five phases of the election process follow. The appendixes offer supplemental facts and figures.

☆ 2 ☆

THE POLITICAL FRAMEWORK
The Parties

All persons elected president since George Washington have run with the support of one of the two major parties of the period. In fact, the need to support the election of an independent national executive was a main impetus behind the rise of national parties. Once they were established, they continued to shape the process by which presidents were chosen.

THE ROLE OF THE PARTIES[1]

Political parties perform a number of basic functions. Seen from the viewpoint of the voter, parties help clarify issues, relate candidates to these issues and simplify the choices the citizen must make in elections. In addition, parties give some coherence to government and give the citizen a basis for judging that government and holding it accountable for its acts. Without parties, citizens would have to find their way with little assistance through a confusing maze of issues, candidates and government actions. Seen from the viewpoint of political leaders, parties are the link among the three branches of the federal government and among local, state and federal governments. They are also the means whereby party supporters are identified and mobilized behind candidates and programs. To use a familiar concept, parties are "brokers"

that help to translate the wishes of people into government policy.

The American Constitution predates the rise of political parties; the document, therefore, makes no mention of them. Although now regulated by federal and state law, parties have developed entirely as extraconstitutional bodies. As early as the 1790s, parties began to control the electoral college system and soon were exercising influence on all elections. Today, most federal and state officeholders, and many local ones as well, are chosen on a partisan basis. Despite this long history of party control of American politics, a popular belief in the desirability of being "nonpartisan" persists, based in part on an association (sometimes correct) of parties with "spoils" and corruption.

From the beginning, American politics has been dominated by two major parties. However, the constituencies of these parties have changed considerably over the years as some groups have moved from one party to another and new groups have been incorporated. The Democratic-Republicans of the Jefferson era were succeeded by the Democrats of Jackson's time, and that party continues today. The Federalists were followed by the Whigs, and the remnants of these groups, as well as new groups, were incorporated into the Republican party under Lincoln. For more than a hundred years, the Democratic and Republican parties have regularly contested national elections.

Traditionally the United States has had a two-party system rather than a multiparty system because our electoral processes have fostered it. In the past 20 years or so, however, some political analysts have questioned whether the two major political parties effectively address the needs and wants of voters and if they can appeal to virtually all segments of American society as they once did. Even before Vietnam, before Watergate, before recent economic recessions, significant numbers of voters were identifying themselves as independents (although they were not necessarily voting that way).

Two-party politics has also been modified by other factors. Distrust and cynicism have enlarged the numbers of political nonparticipants, for example. The 1980 elections saw an accelerated rise in the number and type of extraparty, single-issue groups that played a role in state elections, in some congressional races and in the presidential election itself. Such groups have demonstrated an ability to raise large amounts of campaign money and thus to have an impact on some election results.

There is considerable disagreement over what all this will mean for the American two-party system. Will the future bring a realignment[2] of constituents within the two major parties? Will it mean an entirely new

party taking the place of the Democratic or Republican party? Or will it bring, more drastically, a breakdown into a multiparty system? Even those observers who think the two-party system will survive admit that the events of the last 20 years have profoundly influenced how voters respond to the political system.

PARTY STRUCTURE

The major party organizations have at least four, sometimes five, distinct geographical tiers. The precincts are the bottom layer. At the top stands the figure of the chair of the national committee.

The titular heads of the parties are the president and the defeated nominee of the other party. But their positions are of varying importance in party organization. Some presidential candidates, for example, have had little party influence during the four years following their defeat at the polls. After his second-term loss in 1980, for example, former President Carter chose not to play a visible role in party politics or in affairs of state, thus leaving a void to be filled by half a dozen or more potential 1984 Democratic presidential candidates and the chair of the Democratic National Committee.

Each tier of the party's organization is dependent on the layer below it. In addition, each tier, from precinct to national committee, has its special responsibility within its geographical area in the elections. A common cause, not a chain of command, elicits the necessary cooperation.

The following outline is a skeleton of the structure of the official organization of the two major political parties. The actual situation is far less tidy than this description implies, however. Aside from the national committee, each party does not have a complete working organization at each level, except during election campaigns. Some precincts in some very large cities or even in some counties do not have a full organization for either major party.

Each of these political layers, including those not in the limelight during the nominating conventions, plays a vital role in choosing the nominees for, and in electing, the president and the vice-president.

The Precinct

The precinct, a neighborhood of hundreds of voters, is the basic unit in the political structure and the first theater of operation for party workers.

Some cities also have wards—composed of several precincts. The approximately 175,000 precincts across the country are headed by precinct captains or precinct leaders (other titles are also used). Leaders may be chosen at caucuses, at direct primary elections, or in the general election; or they may be appointed by higher party officials. This precinct executive is the direct link between voters in the precinct and the professional political group. This is the party organization person who, through block workers and other aides, knows a great deal about the individual voters in the precinct and has substantial direct influence on them. Through this leader, the working members of the party at the precinct level, if they work hard in the party and are articulate at the right time and place, may make their voices heard in the selection of delegates.

The County Committee

The county committee, the party tier just above the precinct (in larger cities, just above the ward or district) is a unit of major significance in the party machinery. The chairperson represents local precinct heads on the state committee. Additionally, he or she is directly responsible for the efforts of precinct officials and local party leaders in getting out the vote on election day. The committee itself consists of precinct officials or alternates. The nation's 3,200-plus counties are important functioning political entities.

The State Committee

The state committee (or state central committee) forms the tier above the county committee. The authority and composition of state committees are usually spelled out in state law. They range in size from a handful of people to hundreds of members. Methods of selection differ widely from state to state. The chief function of state committees is to conduct campaigns through their officers and agents and to help in governing the party. They may also influence the choice of delegates to the national conventions, whatever the official selection process may be. In some cases the state committee still selects some delegates. Where states have conventions to select delegates, the state committee wields great influence. Even in states that select delegates via the primary method, control of the state committee may be extremely important.

The National Committee

The national committee is the top layer of party organization. This committee has representatives, at least one man and one woman, from each state and is of prime importance in the choosing of a president. Its chair is a top-ranking professional politician. Its powers and duties are dictated by the national convention.

"Kingpin of the national organization,"[3] the national committee chair is theoretically elected by the national committee but in practice is designated, immediately after the national convention, by the party's presidential candidate.

National committee members may be described as top politicians in their states. They are selected by the states, by a variety of methods. Two of the most common ways are election by the state convention and election by the state's delegates to the national convention. In a number of states, committee members are elected by the voters in the primary, and some state committees appoint the national members. They are often wealthy, because membership on the national committee is costly in both time and money. Many combine experience in law, business and politics.

The national committee members may be the unquestioned statewide party leaders, or their power may emanate from a densely populated area in the state. They may be close aides of the party leaders, or they may be getting their reward for generous contributions of money or for years of party service or distinction.

Apart from its internal structure, each party also has a Senate Campaign Committee and a Congressional Campaign Committee, selected in each new Congress at conferences of party members. These committees raise funds and help in the campaigns of candidates for the Senate and the House of Representatives.

OTHER POLITICAL GROUPS

In addition to the regular party organization in the United States, there are many auxiliary political groups, outside the formal party structure, that supplement the work of the party. There are those that appeal to special segments of the party membership—the National Federation of Republican Women and the Young Democrats, for example. Some groups are splinter groups or factions within the parties and may represent dissatisfaction with the leadership.

Other political groups or committees are mandated by law. The Federal Election Campaign Act, for example, requires that candidates for president who either receive more than $5,000 in contributions or spend more than $5,000 within a campaign cycle name a principal campaign committee through which all contributions to the candidate's campaign chest and all expenditures made in the candidate's name must be reported to the Federal Election Commission. These committees are not part of the regular party structure but are official committees tied to the individual candidate. Some knowledgeable observers point out that the FECA mandate to set up these independent committees outside the regular party apparatus may work to increase the fragmentation of American political parties.

Third Parties and Independent Candidates

Although American politics has been dominated by two major parties, "third" or minor parties have also played an important role in the party system.[4] They flourish whenever the electorate is deeply divided over issues, producing a vociferous minority. In the past, for example, conflicts over how to achieve integration were catalysts for the reemergence of third parties.

The Republican party was once a third party; the Populist party scarred the major parties in the 1890s; Theodore Roosevelt formed the "Bull Moose" party in the 1912 election; and in 1924 the Progressives, led by Robert M. La Follette, Sr., of Wisconsin, got 17 percent of the popular vote by addressing the issue of corporate domination.

In a few states there are third parties that are important at the state level but do not compete for national office; nonetheless, by forming coalitions they can wield considerable influence. In 1970 the Conservative party candidate, James L. Buckley, won the U.S. Senate race in New York.

In 1976 former Minnesota Sen. Eugene J. McCarthy ran for president as an independent, but he lacked the funds, the national constituency and the campaign organization to mount a strong candidacy. In 1980 John Anderson failed to gain the Republican party nomination and then presented himself to the electorate as an independent candidate.

In the modern political era only once has a third party come close to winning the 17 percent of the popular vote scored by La Follette in 1924. In 1968 the American Independent party, led by Governor Wallace of Alabama, attracted 13.5 percent of the total popular vote, thereby winning more electoral votes than any third-party nominee in more than a century.

In 1912, when Teddy Roosevelt decided to run for president on the ''Bull Moose'' ticket against incumbent William Howard Taft, left, he split the Republican vote, thereby paving the way for the election of Democrat Woodrow Wilson, below.

★ 3 ★

THE POLITICAL FRAMEWORK
The Voters

The efforts of the political parties and related political groups all point toward one objective—to bring to the polls on election day voters who will support their candidates. These voters, often referred to as the electorate, form the second major part of the political framework for American presidential elections.

THE EXPANSION OF THE SUFFRAGE

The founding fathers did not have universal adult suffrage in mind as the power base of American government, even though they were opposed to arbitrary rule and had faith in popular sovereignty. In fact, in the earliest years of our democracy, with few exceptions voting was the exclusive province of white males who "had a stake in society" (owned property). By 1850, however, almost all the states had extended the right to vote—at least to all adult free males. Gradually, through constitutional amendment and by federal and state law, the base of democracy has widened and the country has moved steadily in the direction of universal adult suffrage.

Since general voting qualifications were left to the states by the federal Constitution, constitutional amendments and federal statutes have often been employed to expand the electorate. States still set

voting qualifications, but they may not deny the franchise because of race (Fifteenth Amendment) or sex (Nineteenth Amendment). The most recently ratified amendment, the Twenty-Sixth, provides that anyone 18 years of age or over may not be denied the vote on the grounds of age. In addition, the Seventeenth Amendment allowed everyone to vote directly for United States senators for the first time, the Twenty-Third allowed residents of the District of Columbia to vote for president and the Twenty-Fourth banned payment of a poll tax as a requirement for voting. Currently before the states for ratification is an amendment that would allow residents of the District of Columbia full voting representation in the Senate and House. These constitutional changes, together with early action by the states abolishing the initial property restrictions, have had the effect of legally extending the eligibility to vote to all citizens 18 years of age and over. (See Appendix D for text of amendments.)

Carrie Chapman Catt, second from right, and Dr. Anna Howard Shaw, in academic robes, lead a group of suffragists in a New York City parade in 1917 to gain support for woman suffrage. The constitutional amendment granting women the right to vote was ratified by the required number of states on August 26, 1920, at which time the National American Woman Suffrage Association was dissolved and the League of Women Voters was formed in its place.

VOTER TURNOUT AND PROCEDURAL PROBLEMS

Being *eligible* to vote, of course, is not the same as voting. Despite enfranchisement of people on a *group* basis, many *individuals* still do not vote. More people vote in presidential elections than in any other American election, yet even here the turnout since 1960 has rarely exceeded the 1960 level of 62.8 percent of the voting-age population and is often lower. In 1972 about 12 million registered voters failed to vote; about 33 million eligible voters did not even register. In 1976, only 54.3 percent of America's eligible voters turned out. In 1980, this figure dropped slightly to 53.2 percent. See the chart below for voter turnout over the years.

VOTING TURNOUT
in Elections for President
and House of Representatives, 1952-1982

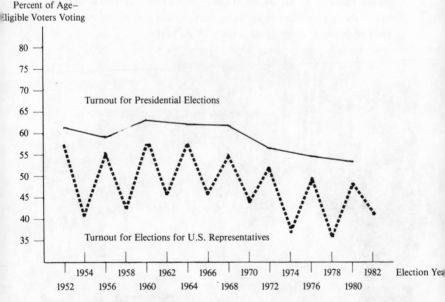

Source: U.S. Census Bureau and David B. Hill and Norman R. Lutt-beg, *Trends in American Electoral Behavior* (F.E. Peacock Publishers, Inc., Itasca, Illinois, 1983), p. 87. Used by permission.

Voting has never been compulsory in the United States as it is in some other countries. Therefore, turnout depends on a wide range of motivating factors—voters' perceptions of candidates, issues and parties as well as their sense of civic responsibility, their estimates of how effective government is, even their feelings of economic or physical safety. Still other factors keep people away from the polls—poor health, inadequate information about where and how to vote, local barriers to registration and voting and transportation problems.

Apathy and dislike of politics in general or of the specific candidates in particular are also reflected in these voting trends. Some traditionally active voters may join the ranks of the younger, poorer and less educated in turning away from the polls because they think their vote would not make much difference or because they do not care about a particular election.

Even though the record of the United States in voter turnout is not as good as it could be, the U.S. turnout rate is perhaps unfairly criticized when it is compared to rates of other Western democracies. Many other countries use a system of government-initiated universal registration, whereas the U.S. system places the initiative for registering on the voter. Also, high voting turnout in some countries is the inevitable result of compulsory voting laws.

In the past, U.S. voter turnout has been adversely affected by procedural roadblocks that some citizens have encountered on the way to the voting booth. At the end of the 19th century various kinds of requirements were established for those seeking to exercise voting eligibility. They included lengthy residence requirements in states and precincts, registration deadlines far in advance of elections, poll taxes, long and complicated literacy tests, proof of good moral character and frequent reregistration requirements. While advocates of many of these processes claimed that such steps were necessary to prevent voting fraud, in fact, the impact was to depress electoral participation. The requirements constituted hurdles that voters had to conquer, and the effects were generally felt most heavily by minorities and by those with less education. Added to this was the fact that election day often meant lines of people waiting to vote and long and confusing ballots. Traditionally, voting turnout was smallest in the Deep South, where income levels were lowest, registration procedures most cumbersome and racial discrimination most obvious.

In recent years, most of these burdensome procedures have been abolished or at least eased. The Twenty-Fourth Amendment in 1964

banned poll taxes in federal elections, and Supreme Court action out-lawed such taxes in state elections. More recently, many states have improved their registration procedures. Twenty states and the District of Columbia now have registration by mail, and four states have a form of election-day registration. Neighborhood and mobile registration sites are increasingly common, as are evening and Saturday hours for voter registration offices. Although the turnout rate has not increased nation-wide, some observers maintain that it would be even lower had it not been for procedural improvements.

THE VOTING RIGHTS ACT

The Voting Rights Act is a complex and detailed law, but its basic intent is simply put: to ensure that racial and language minority citizens, wherever they live, have the same opportunity as other Americans to participate in the nation's political life. To that end, the law, as amended, contains permanent, *general* provisions that apply to the whole country and temporary, *special* provisions that are triggered by the proven existence of discrimination in individual jurisdictions. Basi-cally, the general provisions:

—ensure that length-of-residence requirements will not prevent any citizen from voting in presidential elections;
—prohibit anyone from denying an eligible citizen the right to vote or from interfering with or intimidating anyone seeking to register to vote;
—forbid the use of literacy tests or other devices as qualifications for voting in any federal, state, local, general or primary election.

When the law was first passed in 1965 and again when it was reauthorized and expanded, Congress recognized that special enforce-ment measures were needed to guarantee compliance by state and local governments with a history of officially sanctioned discrimination. The law now contains three "triggers" that are designed to identify such past system-wide bias. The first trigger brings a jurisdiction under special coverage if (1) in the 1964 or 1968 presidential election that jurisdiction had a registration rate or voter turnout of less than 50 percent *and* maintained a test or device (such as a literacy test) as a prerequisite for voting.

In 1975, minority language provisions were added to the Voting Rights Act to ensure that U.S. citizens are not deprived of the right to

vote because they cannot read, write or speak English. A jurisdiction is covered by the language-minority provisions (triggers two and three) if (2) in November 1972 more than 5 percent of the voting-age population in that jurisdiction were members of a single language minority,[1] *and* the jurisdiction provided English-only election materials, *and* less than 50 percent of the voting-age population registered or voted in the 1972 presidential election; or (3) more than 5 percent of the voting-age population in a jurisdiction are members of a single language minority *and* the illiteracy rate for that minority population is higher than the national illiteracy rate. (Illiteracy is defined as failure to complete the fifth grade.)

The original trigger (1) first brought under special coverage the entire states of Alabama, Alaska, Georgia, Louisiana, Mississippi, South Carolina and Virginia, plus approximately 40 counties in North Carolina and scattered counties in Arizona, Hawaii and Idaho. Later a few other localities in other states were added.

During the first years of the act, special coverage primarily meant that the federal government could send *examiners* to register new voters and *observers* to monitor how elections were conducted. Hundreds of such agents were dispatched to oversee and carefully watch compliance procedures.

The actual presence of federal officials is rarely needed now (although federal observers were sent to Mississippi in 1983), but other elements of special coverage have in turn assumed more importance. Those jurisdictions covered under the second or third triggers, for example, must conduct their elections in the appropriate minority language(s) as well as English (but those jurisdictions brought in under the third trigger are not subject to any of the other special provisions).

Section 5 of the act requires jurisdictions under special coverage to submit in advance any proposed change in election laws or procedures—no matter how minor—to the federal government for approval. The intent is to prevent new discriminatory practices from replacing old ones—a common cycle before 1965.

After a long and sometimes acrimonious legislative process, the 1982 amendments to the Voting Rights Act were signed into law shortly before the temporary provisions of the laws were due to expire. The third and strongest extension of the original act, the 1982 amendments modify the special enforcement provisions in Section 5 by providing for standards that must be met by a jurisdiction to "bail out" of special coverage. For the first time, jurisdictions can apply to be removed (or

bailed out) even though their state as a whole does not qualify for removal.

Also, the amendments take into account a 1973 Supreme Court decision *(White* v. *Regester)* that clarifies standards by which minority citizens can prove that their right to participate in the political process has been violated. Finally, effective January 1, 1984, blind, disabled and illiterate persons are entitled to receive assistance at the polls by persons of their choice except the voter's employer or employer's agents or union representatives.

Even with these laws on the books, the difficulty experienced by minorities in registration and political participation remains a reality in many jurisdictions. Threats of economic intimidation, patronizing treatment and laggard service to minority registrants continue to be all too familiar occurrences. In many states the law requires citizens to appear in person to register. Some election officials refuse to allow minority groups to assist in registration drives even though they afford that right to other citizen organizations. At-large elections that dilute minority voting strength are still prevalent. Voting is still held by many officials to be a privilege and not a right.

Congress has in recent years considered measures to encourage greater voter turnout. Since 1970, various proposals for national voter registration by mail have surfaced on Capitol Hill from time to time, but none has passed. An election-day registration bill for federal elections proposed by President Carter also failed to make it through Congress. Although federal legislators express concern about elections and the election process, they have so far deferred in most matters to state authority to run elections. Congress has, however, been more willing to act where basic voting rights are concerned. In addition to the Voting Rights Act, laws passed by Congress have made absentee registration and voting easier for military personnel and their families and for American citizens living overseas.

VOTER BEHAVIOR

Why people vote as they do has always been of interest to scholars, to candidates, to the media and to the people who conduct polls or manage campaigns. Analysis of voting statistics and public opinion polls offers some tentative answers to perennial questions about voting patterns.[2]

Researchers on voting behavior point to three broad factors as being extremely important in influencing a voter's choice: partisan identifica-

tion, issue preferences and candidate preferences. Party affiliation has long been regarded as a major influence among the three, but during the 1970s issues assumed more importance in elections. Also, voters' personal reactions to candidates, including assessment of leadership capabilities and responses to candidate images, are sometimes significant.

Still, a political bench mark to keep in mind is that two-thirds of Americans are partisans—they identify with one of the two major parties. Over the past ten years the number of Americans who identify themselves as Democrats has ranged from 38 to 44 percent; Republicans have ranged from 21 to 24 percent and independents from 30 to 37 percent. In 1982, Americans identified themselves as 44 percent Democratic, 24 percent Republican and 30 percent independent. The party identification chart gives such data from 1952 to 1980.

PARTY IDENTIFICATION

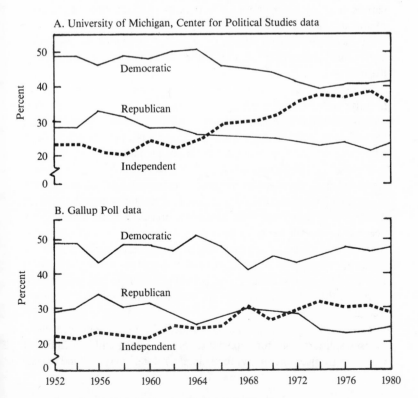

A. University of Michigan, Center for Political Studies data

B. Gallup Poll data

Source: James L. Sundquist, *Dynamics of the Party System* (Brookings Institution, Washington, D.C., 1983), p. 395. Used by permission.

The percentage of independents has recently decreased somewhat after a spurt of growth from 1972 through 1980. Over a 30-year period, however, the proportion of independents has increased greatly from its low base of 22 percent in 1952. While many believe that it is good to be an "independent voter," independents actually dilute their voting effectiveness in many states because they have no voice in the process of nominating candidates through party primaries or caucuses. Studies show that the voter turnout record of independents falls below that of Democrats and Republicans.[3]

No matter what their political orientation, the overwhelming majority of voters seldom think of themselves in terms of "liberal" or "conservative." They respond instead to particular issues, a trend that has become increasingly important in influencing how the vote choice is made.

Another facet of voting behavior to be recognized is that groups sometimes tend to vote in certain ways. Blacks, who represent about 20 percent of the Democratic party's presidential electorate, tend to be the party's most loyal supporters and have on the whole backed Democratic candidates in the last five presidential elections.[4] A recent trend is the increasing tendency for women to identify themselves as Democratic voters, reversing the 1950s trend when women tended to vote Republican.

The personal qualities of candidates also influence voting behavior heavily, sometimes overriding the pull of both party and issues. President Eisenhower's popularity is considered the prime example. Voters also relate to politics on the basis of demographic factors such as their education, ethnic background, occupation, income and religion.

Democratic-Republican divisions in the voting public do not necessarily result in elections determined by those margins. Although only approximately one-fourth of the public is Republican, Republican candidates have won five of the last eight presidential elections, partly because independents have tended to support the Republican presidential candidates in recent elections. Although President Johnson managed to capture 56 percent of the independent vote, President Eisenhower and President Nixon got even higher percentages in their victories. In 1980, 56 percent of independents voted for President Reagan.

Ticket splitting is yet another factor that is becoming more prevalent. (Ticket splitters vote for a president of one party, and a member of Congress from another party, for example.) Voters may respond to state

or local issues and candidates independently of presidential issues and candidates, or they may have strong emotional ties to a party at the local level but not at the national level. Perhaps the most startling example of the ticket-splitting phenomenon occurred in 1972. For the first time in history, a president was elected with more than 60 percent of the popular vote without his party's gaining seats in the House and Senate or winning a majority in either congressional or gubernatorial elections. Despite the growing numbers of ticket splitters and independents, however, party identification is still believed to be a strong determinant of how a voter will cast a ballot.

Overall knowledge of voter behavior helps in predicting political trends and group voting patterns over a period of years. But it cannot be used to reliably forecast winners in every election or to predict the voting choices of an individual.

☆ 4 ☆

THE PRELIMINARIES

The three years or so that elapse between actual presidential campaigns are not a respite from presidential politics but preliminaries to the main event. The political events that occur during this preliminary period will vary, depending upon whether the persons involved are members of the in-party (the party that controls the presidency) or the out-party, or parties.[1] However, all parties and all prospective candidates have to do three essential things in this period: establish a record that will make candidacy possible (although this usually begins years before); develop a power base from which a candidacy can be launched; and devise a strategy to obtain the convention delegate support necessary to win the nomination.

IN-PARTY PRELIMINARIES

The decisions of all prospective candidates in the in-party are heavily affected by the fact that a member of their party is in the White House. Historically, incumbent presidents have been hard to defeat in an election, and it has been considered nearly impossible to wrest the nomination away from them if they want it. For 1984, it was generally understood that Ronald Reagan could have the Republican nomination if he were available and wanted to run. Looking back, however, it is generally condeded that Eugene McCarthy's strong showing in the 1968

New Hampshire Democratic primary greatly influenced President Johnson's decision not to seek his party's renomination. In 1976 Ronald Reagan's challenge to President Ford's Republican candidacy also upset historic precedent. Many observers thought that Ford's apparent vulnerability could be attributed to his being the first nonelected president in our history. Appointed to the vice-presidency before becoming president, he had never run for either office. While Reagan's strategy was unsuccessful at the time, it set the stage for his nomination four years later and his eventual victory over President Carter in 1980.

Sitting presidents have only rarely been denied renomination if they sought it. In fact, those who were not renominated by their parties had succeeded to the top slot from the vice-presidency upon the death of the president. The presidents rejected for their parties' renomination were John Tyler in 1844, Millard Fillmore in 1852, Andrew Johnson in 1868 and Chester A. Arthur in 1884.

Whether a president seeks reelection or not, however, it is his presidential record that the in-party will carry into the next campaign. From a political standpoint a president must build a legislative, executive and diplomatic record that will stand his party in good stead. Policy promises must be kept and political commitments fulfilled. Especially important to the in-party is the midterm election in which all House seats and a third of the Senate seats are filled. Historically, the in-party loses congressional seats in the midterm election. If losses are too heavy, they will be interpreted as a repudiation of the president and his policies, so he has to work to minimize losses and maintain party morale. As the presidential election year approaches, he must pay even more attention to the likely political impact of his actions.

The presidency is the best power base from which to launch a candidacy. If the incumbent does not seek reelection, other candidates must use whatever sources of strength they have. In modern times, the vice-presidency seems to be a good spot for gaining a nomination, but not a particularly good one for winning an election. A vice-president has the advantage of executive experience, media attention and presidential support, but on the other hand he is stuck with the presidential record for better or worse. Since experience has shown that disunity is fatal, he must stand with the record and perhaps fall with it, as Vice-President Humphrey did in 1968. Governors, senators and perhaps a former candidate may also come to the fore if the president steps down.

If a president decides to seek another term, his strategy during the preliminary period will be simple: maintain party harmony and make

sure he controls enough party machinery to ensure that the convention will be a mere formality, renominating him by acclamation and stoutly defending his policies. In the past, the decision of whether to dump an incumbent vice-president came at a later stage. Nelson A. Rockefeller's vow early in the 1976 race not to run with Ford may have set a new pattern.

If a president steps down, other contenders will have many decisions to make: when to announce their candidacy, how heavily to lean on the president in winning delegates, how to use presidential primaries, etc. In 1968 Sen. Robert F. Kennedy tried to win nomination through the primary route; Sen. Eugene McCarthy mounted an extensive grass-roots campaign effort; Vice-President Humphrey worked behind the scenes with presidential support. By and large, in-party strategies are determined by circumstances, the most important of which is the position taken by the incumbent president.

OUT-PARTY PRELIMINARIES

Presidential contenders in the out-party (or parties) are in a position quite different from that of their in-party counterparts and may even have an advantage if the president does not seek reelection. Since they have not been responsible for broad legislative programs, executive actions or diplomatic initiatives, they can criticize presidential efforts in all areas. Even if the out-party controls the Congress, an individual aspirant cannot be held to account because the out-party does not usually develop a broad legislative program of its own, responding instead to presidential actions.

To be sure, a presidential hopeful must build a creditable *individual* record. A governor or mayor who is a contender will, of course, have a public record. But records can be, and often are, more in the nature of promises than accomplishments.

To build a record at all, an out-party aspirant needs a power base. Although candidacies are sometimes launched from appointive positions (Eisenhower in 1952), or private law practice (former Vice-President Mondale in 1984), an elective office is considered best. A party's "titular leader" (usually the most recent losing presidential candidate) will probably try to gain such a position as soon as possible. After 1968, Humphrey sought and won his old Senate seat from Minnesota at the first opportunity; after 1972, George McGovern concentrated on retaining his Senate seat from South Dakota.

Because of the power and prestige of the position and the modern importance of international affairs, the Senate, rather than state or local government, in recent years has been a good place for individuals with presidential ambitions. In 1976, however, candidates from many different arenas emerged. Of the 11 announced Democratic presidential contenders at the start of the campaign season only four were senators, and a fifth was a former senator. Of the six other candidates, two were former governors, two were sitting governors, one was a U.S. representative and one was a former Democratic vice-presidential nominee.

Early in the 1984 campaign Sen. Edward Kennedy, who had mounted an unsuccessful attempt to wrest the nomination from President Carter in 1980, announced that he would not seek the Democratic nomination. A field of contenders then emerged that included four senators—Alan Cranston of California, John Glenn of Ohio, Gary Hart of Colorado and Ernest Hollings of South Carolina—as well as former presidential candidate George McGovern, former Vice-President Mondale and former Ambassador and Governor Reubin Askew of Florida. Additionally, black activist Jesse Jackson announced his candidacy.

In the earliest stages of the "prelims," contenders try to build a favorable image in the party and in the country by making frequent public speeches and appearances at party functions. If prospects seem bright and financial backing emerges, this period of active "noncandidacy" will be followed by a formal announcement. The FECA discourages the formerly common practice of front-runners waiting until the last minute to announce their entry into the race. Limits on the size of campaign contributions mean that those who start raising money early have an advantage.

In the past, some contenders did not engage in preliminary campaigning at all but waited to be "drafted." These drafts were rarely genuine; rather, they were matters of strategy.[2]

The recent proliferation in the number of primaries, straw votes and caucuses—1984 continues a trend—makes the possibility of draft candidates unlikely. Also, the announced intention of the AFL-CIO to back a Democratic candidate early in the 1984 election cycle worked to deter any genuine draft movement in the Democratic party, since labor traditionally influences large numbers of delegates to the Democratic convention.

Although some contenders use a middle-of-the-road appeal to broaden their base of support, others seek backing from particular special-interest groups. For example, Senators Hart and Cranston began

their respective quests for the 1984 nomination by appealing to advocates of a nuclear freeze. Aside from that issue, however, the preliminary period in the 1984 campaign for the Democratic nomination saw only shades of differences between the hopefuls. Most were united in their opposition to the Republican administration's stands on social issues, the economy, defense spending and the environment. In such circumstances, potential convention delegates would need to evaluate a candidate's potential to defeat the in-party rather than base a decision on ideological or issue grounds.

The contenders must make a political decision whether to make a vigorous attack on the presidential record during the campaign. This choice is usually dictated by a contender's past record in this regard and by the current popularity of the incumbent. When a president's popularity ebbs, contenders are more inclined to play on antigovernment themes, as was the case in the 1976 and 1980 contests.

The final strategy decision centers on how to build delegate strength for the nominating convention. At this point, some of the earlier hopefuls will have withdrawn because they failed to get enough money or other support, and the field will be left to those with the most serious chances of success.

THE MEDIA IN THE PRELIMINARIES

The mass media, particularly television and the national newspapers and magazines, play an important role in the preliminary stage of presidential elections.[3] They can virtually create a front-runner by giving exposure or by declaring that the candidate is the front-runner. If they do not take a candidacy seriously, it will be much harder for the contender to raise money and capture early delegate commitments. Obviously, a president who is a candidate has great advantages in media access. The president is news and gets coverage accordingly, and it seems impossible to nullify this built-in advantage. In recent years the out-party has tried (with only limited success), to get air time to reply to broadcasted presidential statements of a partisan flavor. However, the networks have provided the opposition party with prime time to respond to the incumbent president's State of the Union address.

Charges of bias in the media are common and come from all sides. One of Vice-President Agnew's first "official" acts was to denounce the media for their handling of President Nixon's program. Governor Wallace regularly complained that the media distorted his views.

During the 1972 campaign, Sen. Edmund Muskie of Maine bitterly protested the way the press treated him; after his famous "emotional" scene outside the offices of the *Manchester Union Leader* newspaper, some political commentators who covered the campaign say Muskie never regained his stature as a credible candidate. On the other hand, a member of the 1976 Carter staff argued that Carter's *unfavorable* press coverage meant that he was finally being taken seriously.

Rep. Shirley A. Chisholm, the first black woman to seek the presidential nomination, was never really taken seriously by the press. The political clout she developed during the 1972 campaign was surprising to most political commentators, yet most members of the press corps did not mention that she might pose a threat to other better-known liberal candidates.

Even incumbents are sensitive to the make-or-break powers of the media in the early stages of campaigning, when most of the jockeying for support goes on. In early 1976, President Ford seemed to feel he was "under the gun" from the press. According to president-watcher David Broder of the *Washington Post*, Ford responded by striking a "defiant" pose and staunchly defending some of his more controversial policies.

Early in the 1984 campaign, Democratic contenders and Republican President Reagan alike began the traditional rounds of appearances before key groups. Such appearances are designed not only to appeal to particular interests but also to draw the attention of the media to campaign strategies and policy statements.

☆ 5 ☆

CAMPAIGN FINANCING

When politicians say that "Money is the mother's milk of politics," they are speaking the truth. Campaigns and elections are expensive, and costs have escalated greatly. Money is essential to political activity, whether we like it or not.

More than one billion dollars was spent in the 1980 election period on elections and campaigning throughout the United States, including campaigns for the presidency, congressional offices and state and local offices throughout the nation. The 1980 costs of electing a president came to $275 million (primaries, conventions and general election). Campaign finance expert Herbert Alexander maintains that the cost of campaigning is relative, pointing out that a billion dollars is "a fraction of 1 percent of the amounts spent by federal, state, county and municipal governments. . . . It is . . . less than the combined annual advertising budgets of Proctor & Gamble and Sears, Roebuck & Company, the nation's leading advertisers."[1]

Presidential candidates need money to pay for television and radio time, air travel, computers and consultants to do polling and direct mail to solicit voter support. In addition, there are the costs of operating telephone networks to communicate with voters and obvious staff and office costs associated with campaign activities. In an electronic age, presidential candidates are in a more competitive position if they have at

least some access to all these capacities, and they are handicapped if they do not.

Presidential campaign spending has increased greatly in recent years. Alexander notes that in 1968, presidential campaign spending totalled $91 million. In 1972, it was $137.8 million; in 1976 it totalled $159.7 million; whereas in 1980, the bottom line was $275 million. (In the latter two election years, the totals include independent expenditures made on behalf of candidates as well as other campaign spending for presidential elections.)

THE 1971 FEDERAL ELECTION CAMPAIGN ACT

The Federal Election Campaign Act (FECA) of 1971 was the first major overhaul of federal campaign legislation since the Federal Corrupt Practices Act of 1925. The 1971 act, as it applied to presidential or vice-presidential candidates, limited contributions by any candidate, or members of the candidate's immediate family, to the candidate's own campaign, to a maximum of $50,000. It also established a spending limit for media advertising in presidential campaigns, a provision that was repealed in 1974. It specified per-voter spending limits in presidential campaigns before the nominating convention.

The FECA act also provided for disclosure of contributions and expenditures and required the establishment of political committees for organizations that anticipated spending in excess of $1,000. It provided that enforcement of the act would be by the Clerk of the House and the Secretary of the Senate for congressional candidates and by the Comptroller General for presidential candidates.

The 1971 act also provided that radio and television broadcasters could charge political candidates only the lowest unit cost for the same advertising time as might be available to commercial advertisers. This lowest unit rule still applies, but only in the immediate preelection periods.

The FECA changed existing federal prohibitions on direct corporate and labor union contributions to campaigns by providing that such prohibitions did not forbid the establishment of, administration of and solicitation of voluntary contributions to separate, segregated funds to be used for political purposes by labor unions and by corporations.

At the same time, Congress also amended the tax laws to establish the Presidential Election Campaign Fund. This provision allows taxpayers to contribute to the Presidential Campaign Fund for all eligible pres-

idential and vice-presidential candidates in the general election, through a $1 checkoff on the federal income tax form ($2 for joint returns). Approximately 25 to 30 percent of taxpayers avail themselves of this opportunity, a choice that does not increase their tax liability. This provision also allowed taxpayers to claim a tax credit or deduction[2] for contributions to candidates for local, state or federal office.

Congress also established a formula for distributing presidential campaign funds to both major party candidates and minor and new party candidates. The 1971 act forbade major party candidates who chose public financing from accepting private contributions.

THE 1974 AMENDMENTS

Public disclosures during the Watergate investigations of illegal and "laundered" cash contributions from corporations and wealthy individuals to the 1972 Nixon reelection campaign committee shocked citizens and lawmakers alike. The public reporting requirements of the 1971 act *did not* prevent these very large amounts from being donated to campaign coffers in 1972, but they *did* allow citizens to know for the first time exactly who the donors were and how much they had given to whom.

To prevent further abuses Congress tightened the FECA in 1974. Among other provisions, the 1974 amendments:

—established a six-member, bipartisan Federal Election Commission (FEC) to be staffed by two commissioners appointed by the president, two by the Speaker of the House and two by the president pro tempore of the Senate;
—set individual contribution limits of $1,000 per candidate for each primary, general or runoff election, and a total contribution limit of $25,000 per individual to all federal candidates, per year;
—limited contributions from political committees and national or state party committees to $5,000 per candidate for each election;
—set a limit of $1,000 for expenditures on behalf of a candidate made totally independently of the candidate;
—established a $10 million total spending limit for each qualified major party candidate in a presidential primary race (with per state limits), and a $20 million limit for total spending for each nominee in the general election; these sums are pegged to the consumer price index and in 1980 were $17.7 million for the primary and $29.4 million for the general election;

—gave federal funds of $2 million (augmented each election according to the consumer price index) to each major political party to cover costs of the national nominating conventions;

—set up a system of public matching funds for presidential candidates in primary elections to take effect after the candidate reached a threshold of $100,000, raised in amounts of at least $5,000 per state, in 20 or more states, through individual contributions of $250 or less;

—required candidates to establish a principal committee through which all their contributions and expenditures would be funneled and reported, and also required them to file detailed reports with the FEC; and

—permitted labor unions, government contractors and corporations to establish segregated funds for political purposes only.

BUCKLEY V. VALEO

Within days after the 1974 act was passed, it was challenged in federal court by independent presidential candidate Eugene McCarthy, Conservative-Republican Sen. James Buckley, and General Motors heir and political philanthropist Stewart Mott. In January 1976, the Supreme Court issued a landmark decision in *Buckley* v. *Valeo* by which it tried to balance First Amendment rights against the interests of Congress and the public in reforming the campaign process. Basically, the Court upheld contribution limits and overturned expenditure limits. It outlawed both the limitation on independent expenditures and the limitation on candidates' expenditures on their own behalf as unconstitutional restrictions on the First Amendment rights of political expression.

The Court left in place, however, the overall personal candidate expenditure limits for candidates who accept public funds, ruling that the Congress has the right to attach that condition to the use of public money. Further, it ruled that independent expenditures could not be made in collusion or in coordination with a candidate. These expenditures must be truly independent and spent by an individual or an organization without reference to any campaign or candidate consultation.

The Court upheld the overall limitations on contributions by both individuals and groups to campaign committees, stating that such limitations are acceptable under the Constitution because they serve to dilute the influence of large contributors and prevent undue influence on federal elections.

All the disclosure requirements were upheld by the Court, as were the public funding methods. Also left intact was the *concept* of a bipartisan commission to regulate the campaign finance law, but the Court ruled that, under the constitutional concept of separation of powers, the president has the sole power to appoint the members of the commission, with the advice and consent of the Senate. This decision struck down the system whereby one-third of the commissioners were chosen by the president, one-third by the Speaker of the House and one-third by the president pro tempore of the Senate, as the 1974 law had provided.

The Court gave Congress 30 days (later extended to 50 days) to reconstitute the FEC, but Congress was unable to act within that time. In March 1976, therefore, the Federal Election Commission lost its ability to certify payments of matching funds, causing great concern among candidates during the 1976 primary period. It was not until May of that year that Congress was able to pass a revised law, restructuring the FEC and otherwise making the necessary amendments. After signing it, President Ford then delayed appointing the commissioners for another several days, in effect holding up matching money for contenders in the Michigan and Maryland primaries.

THE 1976 AMENDMENTS

The 1976 amendments to the Federal Election Campaign Act:

—set a limit of $5,000 per year for individual contributions to political action committees and provided that individuals could not give more than $20,000 per year to the national committee of a political party;

—limited multicandidate committees[3] to giving no more than $15,000 a year to the national committee of a political party;

—retained the 1974 contribution limit of $5,000 per election, per candidate, from a multicandidate committee;

—set spending limits of $50,000 of their own or their family's money for presidential candidates who received public funds; and

—established an independent Federal Election Commission, as the Supreme Court had required.

In a significant action, the 1976 law restricted multiple corporate and union political action committees (PACs) from the same parent entity by providing that all PACs established by a company or by a union

would be treated as a single committee for contribution purposes and that no PAC, whether union or corporate, could give more than $5,000 per candidate, per election. (See page 42 for more on PACs.) Further, corporations, unions and membership organizations were restricted from seeking contributions outside their purview. Companies could solicit contributions only from stockholders, executive and administrative staff and families. Unions could solicit contributions only from their members and families. But communications from these separate segregated funds to the general public for the purpose of soliciting contributions were prohibited.

The 1976 amendments also strengthened the enforcement provisions of the Federal Election Commission. Unions, corporations and membership organizations were required to disclose expenditures of more than $2,000 per election used to communicate to their stockholders or members concerning the election or defeat of a federal candidate.

THE 1979 AMENDMENTS

Following the 1976 election, and widespread complaints by parties and candidates about the burden of campaign record-keeping requirements, several changes were made in the law in 1979 to ease the process of compliance with the FECA.

The amendments:

—raised the reporting requirement for federal candidates to a threshold of $5,000 in receipts or expenditures;

—permitted local party organizations to avoid reporting certain voluntary activities valued at less than $5,000 (get-out-the-vote drives, voter registration drives, etc.);

—permitted individuals to spend up to $1,000 on behalf of a candidate in providing voluntary services (use of a home for a meeting, food, travel, etc.) without these being considered contributions to the candidate;

—required that the name of the candidate must appear in all campaign committee titles;

—required frequent reports to the FEC of the names of donors and amounts of donations of $200 or more (instead of the original $100 requirement);

—required the reporting of independent expenditures of $250 or more (instead of the original $100 requirement);

—strengthened the role of political parties by allowing them to

conduct registration or get-out-the-vote drives without limit and to buy promotional products such as bumper stickers, brochures and buttons without limit; and

—allowed the allocation of $3 million in federal funds for the Democratic and Republican nominating conventions rather than the previous $2 million.

POLITICAL ACTION COMMITTEES

Since the passage of the FECA in the early 1970s, campaign spending patterns have been greatly affected by the growth in importance of political action committees (PACs).[4] PACs exist to raise and spend campaign money. With strict federal restrictions on corporate, union and individual contributions to campaigns, PACs have come to be a commonly used and relatively unencumbered way to raise and make political contributions.

"Political action committee" or "PAC" can refer to two types of noncandidate, nonparty political committees under the meaning of the FECA (the term is not mentioned in the law). One refers to "separate, segregated funds"—political committees established by and affiliated with corporations, labor unions, trade membership organizations, co-operatives or corporations without capital stock. The other refers to "nonconnected" political committees.

The "separate, segregated fund" type of PAC developed because of the federal prohibition on direct corporate, national bank and union contributions to candidates for federal office. The FECA made possible a means for separate political committees, organized by and tied to such institutions, to solicit and disburse voluntary contributions to candidates. Such PACs are restricted to communicating with their management, or members, and families, and they may not make solicitations directed at the general public. Such affiliated PACs have the advantage of having their administrative and fund-raising costs borne by the corporation, union or membership association. About 80 percent of all PACs are of this separate, segregated fund type—i.e., tied to the parent entity and accountable to it.

A second type of PAC—perhaps the one more commonly thought of—is the "nonconnected" political committee. These are independent committees whose purpose is to raise and spend money for campaign purposes. Such independent or nonconnected PACs are not bound by the restrictions that bind separate, segregated fund PACs when it comes

to communications and fund raising. Nonconnected PACs can raise funds from the public (most do so by direct mail). They lack the advantage, however, of a parent organization to bear administrative and fund-raising costs.

Both kinds of committees can benefit from qualifying under federal law as multicandidate committees. In doing so, they increase their contribution limit to $5,000 per election per federal candidate (''persons'' are restricted to $1,000).[5] To qualify as a multicandidate committee, a PAC must be registered with the Federal Election Commission for six months, receive contributions from more than 50 persons and make contributions to five or more federal candidates.

A $1,000 contribution limit applies to persons or to organizations and groups unless the organization qualifies as a multicandidate committee. As a result, there is a five-to-one contribution-making advantage for the multicandidate committees, an advantage that experts see as significant to the growth of PACs over the years. Since individuals cannot qualify as such a committee, they are restricted to a $1,000 contribution limit.

Who cares? Why is it important to know about PACs? A look at their growth and impact on campaign spending over time tells the story, and that story points to PACs as major funders of modern-day campaigns. In 1975 there were 608 PACs registered with the FEC. By the end of 1982 there were 3,371. (The FEC believes that yearly increases in the number of PACs since 1976 have averaged about 20 percent; between 1974 and 1976, PAC numbers increased 88 percent.) (See the chart on page 44 for an overview.)

Observers look not only at the growth in numbers of PACs but also at the growth in their receipts and contribution levels. There has been a sharp rise in the *amount* of campaign dollars accounted for by PAC activity, compared to the base level in the early 1970s. In 1980, PAC contributions to congressional candidates totalled $55.2 million and in 1982, $83.1 million, whereas in 1972 the figure was an estimated $8.5 million.[6]

Presidential candidates in the 1980 preconvention period received $1.56 million in direct PAC contributions.[7] Such PAC contributions to primary election candidates cannot qualify for federal matching funds. Candidates in the general election operated under total public financing, and in 1980 the two major party candidates qualified for public funds in the amount of $29.4 million each. So the $1.56 million figure, spread over several candidates in a primary period, should be kept in perspective.

PAC GROWTH

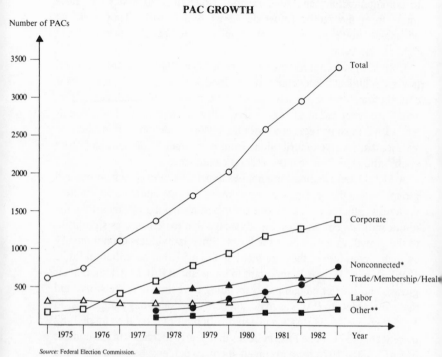

Source: Federal Election Commission.

*For the years 1974 through 1976, the FEC did not identify subcategories of PACs other than corporate and labor PACs. Therefore, numbers are not available for Trade/Membership/Health PACs and Nonconnected PACs.

**Includes PACs formed by corporations without capital stock and cooperatives. Numbers are not available for these categories of PACs from 1974 through 1976.

What the discussion thus far does not reflect is the role played by independent expenditures by PACs—or by individuals, for that matter—in presidential campaigns. Under the law, groups or individuals can spend unlimited dollars to support or oppose federal candidates. The expenditures must be truly independent of a candidate's campaign; no collusion, even tacit, can exist.

In 1980, independent expenditures in the presidential campaign totalled $13.7 million, with $12.5 million spent independently for or against Jimmy Carter and Ronald Reagan.[8] Of this, $11 million was spent during the general election. During both primary and general election periods, independent expenditures for President Carter totalled

$46,000 and against him $246,000. Candidate Reagan, however, attracted $12.2 million in independent expenditures on his behalf—$10.7 million of it during the general election campaign. About $1.7 million of that sum was spent by the National Conservative Political Action Committee (NCPAC), best known for its "negative spending" campaign against certain members of Congress. Another conservative PAC, the Congressional Club, spent $4.1 million on Ronald Reagan's behalf.[9] Independent expenditures against Reagan came to $48,000 overall.

ASSESSING THE FECA

The new method of financing our presidential campaigns has altered our election system in fundamental ways. Large, secret contributions have been outlawed. Contributions and expenditures are now public record. Direct mail campaigns that saturate the country with appeals for small donations have become prominent in campaign fund raising. And PACs have proliferated like dandelions on a spring lawn.

While some changes stemming from the FECA have been predictable, others have been surprising. Traditionally, candidates with the ability to raise money early in the game have had the best chances in the race toward nomination. For many, intensive fund raising took place close to home, but the matching-fund requirements now mean that each presidential contender must set up functioning committees in 20 or more states at the outset of a campaign. In 1976 Terry Sanford chose not to do this and he ran headlong into a quirk that arose from the FECA. The former governor of North Carolina found that until he met the matching-fund requirement, he would not be considered by the press to be a serious contender. He strenuously objected to this "legitimizing" aspect of the law but to no avail, and he dropped out of the campaign early.[10] On the other hand, 1976 candidate Jimmy Carter managed his early financial resources very well, enabling his campaign to spend money early so that he could have a major showing in the critical New Hampshire primary and Iowa caucuses. This achievement gave him early visibility as an important candidate.

The FECA has its supporters and its detractors. More observers than not think that the advent of public financing has greatly strengthened the integrity of the presidential election process. Public financing is volun-

tary, but most presidential candidates have accepted it and the expenditure limitations that such acceptance brings.

One change in the law that many experts have suggested is to increase the individual contribution limit from $1,000 to a higher figure (some suggest $3,000, some $5,000) to make it more nearly equal to the amount that PACs may now contribute to candidates and also to take account of the effects of inflation.

The proliferation and impact of PACs have also raised concern among campaign finance experts. Some point out that the increase in the number of PACs means that there are PACs on all sides of any given issue and that there will be offsetting contributions and expenditures by PACs committed to opposing views on various issues and candidates. However, critics note the tremendous growth in the number of corporate and trade association PACs as a significant change in the pattern of campaign financing. Also of concern is the increasing reliance of members of Congress on funds from special interest groups through PAC contributions.

In addition, many fear that such independent expenditures will not benefit candidates equally and will increase the campaign impact of a given presidential candidate who has extensive independent expenditures made in his behalf. Concerns are based on the 1980 pattern, in which independent PAC expenditures on behalf of Ronald Reagan—$12.2 million—dwarfed the $46,000 spent on behalf of Jimmy Carter. It remains to be seen whether this pattern will be repeated or whether such imbalances were peculiar to the circumstances of the 1980 election. Nevertheless, in view of the Supreme Court's restrictions against limiting independent expenditures, it is difficult to see how the law could be changed without running afoul of Court concerns over First Amendment rights.

Some critics have pointed to the complexities of the law as a detrimental feature, suggesting that campaign finance administration is a growth industry spawning hosts of accountants, lawyers and fund raisers familiar with the sometimes arcane provisions of the law. The legal complexities have led to the increased remoteness of the whole process from the average citizen. Also, it is difficult for candidates to feel secure about compliance when the procedures are so complex.

Criticism has also been directed at the change made in the FECA in 1979 to strengthen the role of political parties. The 1979 amendments permitted the parties to spend without limit for conducting voter registration drives and get-out-the-vote drives and for buying such things as

bumper stickers and brochures. However, money spent in this way relieves the campaign committee of the burden of spending *its* funds for such purposes and permits the campaign to allocate those resources to other uses. This is the so-called "soft money" that has come to be talked of in campaign financing circles—money that can legally be spent outside the prohibitions and requirements of the FECA.[11]

With all the FECA's complexities, it is still fair to say that elections have been more open since its passage. Under the FECA, citizens and the press have had access to more information about who finances campaigns and how the money is spent.

☆ 6 ☆

DELEGATE SELECTION
The
Convention
Game Begins

It is far easier and more exciting to follow candidates on the campaign trail than it is to keep up with the ever-changing rules for the selection of delegates to the national party conventions that nominate presidential candidates. But these rules are crucial factors in candidates' development of campaign strategy. This has been especially true in the 1970s and 1980s because campaign laws and changing party rules have kept the selection process in a state of flux. In an effort to balance demands for an open nominating process with pressures to keep party alliances in place for the upcoming election, the parties, particularly the Democratic party, have developed nominating processes so complicated that even the professionals need a scorecard to keep track of the game.

METHODS OF CHOOSING DELEGATES

State law and party rules combine to govern methods of choosing delegates and to determine whether the caucus/convention method, the primary, or a combination of the two is used as a means of picking each state's delegates. The 1984 Democratic Convention will also seat a number of appointed delegates and state and local elected officials. For the Republicans, the presidential candidate(s) will have an official role in the method of delegate selection in four states (California, Louisiana,

Texas, and Wisconsin). In most states, people who want to be delegates may commit themselves to a specific presidential candidate or they may run uncommitted.

Primaries

In a primary, party voters express their preferences for presidential candidates by voting in an election rather than by attending a meeting or a caucus. Primaries were devised during the reformist era of the early 20th century as one way to take power away from party machines and give the electorate a role in the nominating process. By 1916, 26 states had primary laws on the books, though only some of them applied to the presidential nomination. By 1935, eight states had repealed their primary laws, but after World War II, interest in primaries was revived. Election commentaries often cite the high number of primaries in 1976 and 1980—31 and 36 respectively—as a sign of a growing trend. However, these totals included both binding primaries and advisory or nonbinding "beauty contest" primaries. In 1984, 29 states and the District of Columbia planned to hold primaries (some advisory, some binding). Additionally, other states planned a primary for one major party and a caucus or convention for the other.

The 1984 delegate selection process thus shaped up as a mixture of methods. States not holding primaries to select delegates planned to use caucuses or conventions or a combination of primary and caucus. The delegate selection chart gives details by state. Republicans will select a total of 2,234 convention delegates while Democrats will choose 3,931, plus alternates.

Primary Terminology

To understand news reports and political commentators when they talk about primaries, it helps to have a quick definition of key terms.

• *Open primary:* Permits voting in that primary by any registered voter regardless of party. Such primaries are not favored by party leaders. The Democratic National Committee has ruled that primaries held in open primary states are not binding on the selection of delegates.

• *Closed primary:* Restricts voting in that primary to voters who have registered in advance as being affiliated with that party.

• *Direct presidential preference primary:* Lists all party candidates for presidential nomination on the party ballot. Some preferential primaries are binding, some are advisory. Delegates are selected at a caucus after the primary.

• *Winner-take-all:* All delegates go to the primary winner. In 1984, only the Republican primary in California will be of this type. The Democrats do not permit winner-take-all primaries.

• *Direct delegate selection:* Voters vote for the delegates themselves as listed on the ballot. Generally, the name of the presidential candidate supported by a particular delegate is also listed on the ballot. This makes it easy for voters to coordinate their own presidential preference with their vote for delegates. In 1984, Democratic candidates will have the right of prior approval of all delegates listed as supporting them on the primary ballots.

• *Proportional:* After the voters vote for presidential candidates, the delegates are allotted on the basis of the proportions of the vote won by the various candidates. Distribution may be statewide or in districts (congressional or other) within a state. It may also be partly district, partly statewide.

The Democrats decided to hold most of their 1984 primaries (and caucuses) early in 1984, between the end of February and the end of March. Almost half of the delegates to the nominating convention were scheduled to be selected during this period. Such "front-loading" of the delegate selection process puts a premium on early campaign organization and fund-raising. The remaining Democratic primaries take place up until early June. The Republicans scheduled their primaries to begin in late February and run through early June 1984.

Caucus/Convention

In the caucus/convention method of choosing delegates to national party conventions, those registered in that party, anyone who voted in the last primary, or, in some states, anyone who is willing to sign a pledge that she or he is a bona fide party member, can meet together at the precinct level, usually the county. Party rules require caucus dates, times and places to be publicized in advance. Delegates to county conventions then select representatives to go on to district and state conventions. Usually, prospective delegates' presidential preferences are known or declared; delegates may also run as undecided. In any case, those attending the meetings have a clear knowledge of whom (if anyone) these delegates will back when they reach the national nominating convention.

Under party rules, Democrats must choose their delegates according to proportional representation at each level; that is, delegates selected to go on to the next level must fairly reflect the proportion of support that

each presidential candidate (or the undecided block) has won at the meeting. The Democrats allowed for a new option in 1984, at the statewide level. In some cases, where three or more delegates are to be chosen, one delegate could be allocated to the front-runner, the remaining delegates to be apportioned among the leading contenders. Only nine states opted for such a process; all others used the direct or proportional method. The Democratic rules stipulated that in each state, a candidate must receive a minimum percentage of support in order to be represented.

PARTY REFORM

The delegate selection processes of the political parties were not immune to the political ferment associated with the Vietnam War and civil rights protests of the 1960s, which focused public attention on governmental and political processes. Critics directed attention to the fact that the method of selecting delegates to the nominating conventions of both major parties tended to under-represent women, minorities and young people. Subsequently, both parties undertook reform measures to make delegate selection processes more accessible.

Democrats

The contentious 1968 Democratic National Convention in Chicago, and Hubert Humphrey's defeat by Richard Nixon in the subsequent election, generated demands for reform that were reflected in the 1972 Democratic National Convention delegate selection process. The two most controversial changes were: 1) the encouragement of more participation by, and representation of young people, women and racial minorities by requiring state delegations to represent the proportions of these categories in that state's population; 2) the limiting of the number of delegates selected by state party committees to 10 percent of the total delegation.

For 1976, the Democratic National Committee (DNC) revised the rules governing the selection of delegates to require affirmative action plans. The portion of delegates that state party committees could select was increased from 10 percent to 25 percent. Significant rule changes continued in 1980 when state delegations had to be equally divided between men and women and the time period during which delegates could be chosen was shortened to three months—from the second Tuesday in March to the second Tuesday in June. Only registered

DELEGATE SELECTION, 1984, BY STATE

Key: D = Democrat   R = Republican

The table below lists dates and method of choosing delegates to national nominating conventions, and, in some cases, dates of advisory primaries. For several states, final dates had not been determined as late as the fall of 1983. In the caucus states, where the process extends over a period of days or weeks, the beginning date is generally listed. For questions about particular states, contact the Democratic National Committee or the Republican National Committee, or the state party committees.

State		Number of Delegate Votes	Delegate Selection Method	Date
Alabama	D	62	Primary	March 13
	R	38	Primary	March 13
Alaska	D	14	Primary	March 13[1]
	R	18	Primary	March 13
Arizona	D	39	Caucus	April 14
	R	32	Caucus	May
Arkansas	D	42	Caucus	March 17
	R	29	District Committees	February 4
California	D	345	Primary	June 5
	R	176	Primary	June 5
Colorado	D	51	Caucus	May 7
	R	35	Caucus	May 7
Connecticut	D	60	Primary	March 27
	R	35	Primary	March 27
Delaware	D	18	Caucus	March 14
	R	19	Caucus	Spring 1984
Florida	D	143	Primary	March 13
	R	82	Primary	March 13
Georgia	D	84	Primary	March 13
	R	37	Primary	March 13
Hawaii	D	27	Caucus	March 13
	R	14	Caucus	January 24
Idaho	D	22	Advisory Primary	May 22
			Caucus	May 24
	R	21	Primary	May 22
Illinois	D	194	Primary	March 20
	R	93	Primary	March 20
Indiana	D	88	Primary	May 8
	R	52	Primary	May 8
Iowa	D	58	Caucus	February 20[2]
New Mexico	D	28	Primary	June 5
	R	24	Primary	June 5
New York	D	285	Primary	April 3
	R	136	Primary	April 3
North Carolina	D	88	Primary	May 8
	R	53	Primary	May 8
North Dakota	D	18	Caucus	March 14–28
			Advisory Primary	June 12
	R	18	Caucus	January 15–March 15
			Advisory Primary	June 12
Ohio	D	175	Primary	May 8
	R	89	Primary	May 8
Oklahoma	D	53	Caucus	March 13
	R	35	Caucus	March 5
Oregon	D	50	Primary	May 15
	R	32	Primary	May 15
Pennsylvania	D	195	Primary	April 10
	R	98	Primary	April 10
Rhode Island	D	27	Primary	March 13
	R	14	Primary	March 13
South Carolina	D	48	Caucus	March 17
	R	35	Caucus	February–March
			Primary	March 10 (tentative)
South Dakota	D	19	Primary	June 5
	R	19	Primary	June 5
Tennessee	D	76	Primary	May 1
	R	46	Primary	May 1
Texas	D	200	Caucus	May 5
	R	109	Caucus	June 15

	R	32	Caucus	May–June
Kentucky	D	63	Caucus	March 17
	R	37	Caucus	March 10
Louisiana	D	68	Caucus	April 14
	R	41	Caucus	May 19 (tentative)
Maine	D	27	Caucus	March 4
	R	20	Caucus	February 1–March 15
Maryland	D	74	Primary	May 8
	R	31	Primary	May 8
Massachusetts	D	116	Primary	March 13
	R	52	Primary	March 13
Michigan	D	155	Caucus	March 17
	R	77	Caucus	January 11–12
Minnesota	D	86	Caucus	March 20
	R	32	Caucus	March 20
Mississippi	D	43	Caucus	March 17
	R	30	Primary	June 5
Missouri	D	86	Caucus	April 18
	R	47	Caucus	March 31–April 7
Montana	D	25	Caucus	March 25
			Advisory Primary	June 5
	R	20	Primary	June 5
Nebraska	D	30	Primary	May 15
	R	24	Primary	May 15
Nevada	D	20	Caucus	March 13
	R	22	Caucus	May 3–5
New Hampshire	D	22	Primary	February 28[3]
	R	22	Primary	February 28
New Jersey	D	122	Primary	June 5
	R	64	Primary	June 5
	R	26	Caucus	April 16
Vermont	D	17	Advisory Primary	March 6
			Caucus	April 24
	R	19	Advisory Primary	March 6
			Caucus	April 24
Virginia	D	78	Caucus	March 24 or 26
	R	50	Caucus	June 1 and 2
Washington	D	70	Caucus	March 13
	R	44	Caucus	March 6
West Virginia	D	44	Primary	June 5
	R	19	Primary	June 5
Wisconsin	D	89	Advisory Primary	April 3
			Caucus	April 7
	R	46	Primary	April 3
			Caucus	May 1–June 20
Wyoming	D	15	Caucus	March 10
	R	18	Caucus	February 5–March 5
District of Columbia	D	19	Primary	May 1
	R	14	Primary	May 1
American Samoa	D	6	Caucus	May 13
Democrats Abroad	D	5	Primary (Mail Ballot)	March 13
Guam	D	7	Caucus	April 15
	R	4	Caucus	March–April
Latin American Democrats	D	5	Caucus	March 17
Puerto Rico	D	53	Primary	March 18
	R	14	Primary	February 19
Virgin Islands	D	6	Caucus	April
	R	4	Caucus	April

Sources: Congressional Research Service, Library of Congress; Republican National Committee; Democratic National Committee; and news reports.

1. Caucuses may be scheduled for later in the spring.
2. February 20 is the date preferred by state party officials. However, even as late as December 1983, the Democratic National Committee (DNC) preferred holding caucuses on February 27.
3. March 6 was the date originally approved by the DNC. State party officials preferred an earlier date—February 28. As late as December 1983, negotiations were still going on concerning the date.

Democrats could vote in Democratic primaries, and state delegations had to reflect the proportion of the vote that each candidate received in the primary election or state caucus. To respond to criticisms that earlier reforms had worked to exclude party and elected officials from the process, the number of delegates was increased by 10 percent to allow more elected party and state officials to be included.

After Jimmy Carter's second-term loss in 1980, the Democratic Party set up a Commission on Presidential Nomination, headed by North Carolina Governor James B. Hunt, to take another look at the whole delegate selection question. The Commission was unable to fully achieve one of its stated goals—a shortened campaign season. But it did make substantial changes in the rules designed to lessen the likelihood of a dark-horse candidate capitalizing on the momentum gained by early victories in the Iowa caucuses and the New Hampshire primary. As a result of the Hunt Commission changes, 12 weeks are set aside as the "window" during which all delegate selection must occur. Only days separate the Iowa caucuses from the primary in New Hampshire in 1984. By the end of March, 42 percent of pledged delegates will have been selected compared to 38 percent at the same point in the 1980 campaign.

Republicans

Republicans also responded to the reform sentiment that was prevalent in the late 1960s, although their reforms were more cautious than those of the Democrats. Basically, the Republican rules adopted by the 1976 Convention govern the delegate selection process. Republicans call on state party organizations to take "positive action" to achieve broad participation by women, young people, minorities, "heritage" groups and senior citizens. The Republican National Committee (RNC) urges equal representation of men and women. No mechanism exists to mandate compliance with these standards. Other reforms include a ban on proxy voting and on ex-officio or automatic "senior party official" delegates. Republicans have made efforts to make party meetings more public and visible.

The Republican party operates under a somewhat different set of premises than the Democratic party. Republicans believe that national party leadership must not dictate to state party processes. The result is that the Republican National Committee recommends, but does not require, that reforms and changes be made by the state and local party units to ensure broad-based participation in party processes.

EVALUATING THE SELECTION PROCESS

Both the primary system and the caucus/convention system of choosing delegates to the national conventions have their strong and weak points. Some people wonder whether the primaries have actually achieved the initial goal of democratizing participation in the delegate selection process since voter turnout in primary elections is low compared to turnout in general elections (only about 25 percent of the voting-age population votes in primaries).

It is true that primary elections appeal to highly motivated voters. Scholars have found that the average primary voter tends to be slightly better educated, more affluent and older than the average voter in general elections. Primary voters are also more likely to be interested in a particular candidate or to have strong party ties.

Observers also note that a grueling series of primary elections, extending from the winter of a presidential election year to the summer, places a tremendous drain on candidates and campaign personnel alike, to say nothing of campaign funds. Reformers have long suggested shortening the primary election campaign period to take account of all these problems. Experts feel that the changes in that direction proposed for 1984 can be beneficial.

Supporters of primary elections cite the fact that they offer relatively unknown candidates a chance to build their credibility and to assess their general popularity and intra-party strength, and perhaps to capture the nomination through a series of early primary victories. But others point out that the primary process diminishes the influence in the nominating process of state and local party officials as well as members of Congress, persons who generally have a realistic view of presidential leadership skills. The Democrats have dealt with this by having a 10 percent add-on for *pledged* party and elected officials and an additional add-on for *unpledged* party and elected officials. The unpledged group includes a minimum of three-fifths of the Democratic members of the House and Senate, chosen by their own caucuses.

Critics of the caucus/convention method of selecting delegates to the national convention stress that participation in caucuses/conventions involves an even lower percentage of persons than is the case in primary elections. However, the caucuses at the community level can help to build party unity.

All in all, no one advocates returning to the practices of a past era when smoke-filled rooms and secret deals for deciding presidential nominations were the common *modus operandi*.

☆ 7 ☆

THE
CONVENTION

"Several thousand people, most of them parochial in outlook and strangers to one another . . . thrown together for a few days to make a set of major decisions, under conditions of great strain and maximum publicity."[1] That is how one of the best writers on the subject describes the quadrennial rite of the national political party conventions. Months of state conventions and primaries and years of candidate activity have gone before.

Well in advance of the meeting date, each national committee selects a city for the convention site. Local pride and the prospect of increased business induce many cities to lobby for the honor, and the national committees make their selections on the basis of convenience, available accommodations and political considerations. The sheer size of the conventions limits the sites to those cities with major convention facilities. In 1984, the Democrats will meet July 16–19 in San Francisco, California, and the Republicans will meet August 20–23 in Dallas, Texas.

FUNCTIONS OF NATIONAL CONVENTIONS

National conventions have no formal standing in the election process defined in the Constitution. Without the work done by the conventions,

however, there would be no true national parties. Conventions make their own rules and are the supreme authority over other components of the national parties, including the national committees. They are exercises in power both on and off the convention floor. As we have seen, Democrats maintain strict control over the rules by which delegates are chosen, as well as over committee structure and other internal affairs; Republicans usually leave this type of decision to their state committees. Regardless of the methods used, parties have few ways to enforce their decisions other than to refuse admittance or credentials to a violator at future conventions. In many cases, the lengthy preparations that precede conventions enable differences within the party to be sorted out before they surface on the convention floor.

The convention performs four major functions:

(1) *It nominates candidates for president and vice-president.* Major party nominees can depend on having their names—and/ or a slate of electors pledged to them—on the November election ballot in all states, a luxury not easy for a minor party or independent candidate to come by. Formal nomination by a major party is a practical necessity for candidates because of the existence of a massive, nationwide electorate. Candidates could be nominated in other ways, such as by a state-by-state direct primary, but that method would rob the major national parties of much of their role and influence. Formal major party nomination also qualifies the Republican and Democratic nominees for public funding of their general election campaigns, unless they opt for a privately funded campaign.

(2) *It adopts a national party platform.* Although the platform is not binding on members of the party, it does establish a tone and direction behind which most party members can rally, and it serves a number of other purposes that will be discussed later. After the election, presidents, senators and representatives interpret the platform to suit their own needs and philosophies.

(3) *It governs the party.* Policies and procedures for the next convention are adopted and study groups may be appointed. For Democrats, all state nominations for national committee members must be approved by the national convention, thus providing leadership for the next four years. Republicans rely on state law and/or state party rules in this regard.

(4) *It rallies the party faithful.* It can provide a time for the healing of wounds that may have been opened during the campaign for

nomination and can bring factions together behind a ticket. Up to the time of the convention, contenders have vied for delegate votes; after the convention they must present a united front to win the votes of citizens.

THE GATHERING OF THE DELEGATES

A convention city on the eve of a meeting is a center of activity and expectancy. Delegations are as different from one another as the states they represent. Some hold meetings to choose their leaders—chair, vice-chair and secretary—before they leave home. Others wait until they arrive to take care of these matters. Until modern reforms, delegates were usually upper-middle-class, college-educated, professional or managerial persons; many were professional politicians or elected officials—and most of them were male. Frequently, delegates have had only a limited previous acquaintance with other members of their own delegation.

Soon after arrival, preliminary conferences and caucuses begin. Each state delegation has its own headquarters to direct activities such as meeting with candidates and issuing press releases. Meeting at the same time, and competing with state caucuses for the presence of delegates, are representatives of labor, business, agriculture, religious or other such interests. Many of these groups hope to influence both the choice of candidates and the planks that make up the party platform. Indeed, spokespersons for these groups may have already testified at hearings of the platform committees, held months before.

Television cameras, microphones and other electronic equipment are already in place at the convention hall and in main meeting rooms and hotels. Because of the huge television and radio audience that will be tuned in throughout the convention, each step of the meeting is planned down to the minute, although prolonged credentials arguments, spontaneous demonstrations or other unforeseen circumstances often disrupt the most careful of plans. In 1972, even though strategists had planned for George McGovern to deliver his acceptance speech in prime time (around 10:00 P.M. EST), a floor dispute preceding the speech lasted into the early morning hours. By the time McGovern finally made his speech, most of the television audience had gone to bed.

CONVENTION MAKEUP

Long before convention time each party will have decided how many people—voting delegates or otherwise—will be admitted to the convention and how the total number will be apportioned among the states. This allocation is announced in the "Final Call to Convention" and sent to state and local parties long before the selection process begins.

Critics have often complained that the thousands of people in attendance at conventions make meaningful deliberation impossible. They have recommended smaller conventions with fewer delegate votes and fewer alternates. Most party leaders have argued, however, that there must be enough delegate votes to be representative of the national constituency that makes up the party. Additionally, a smaller convention would reduce the number of faithful workers who look forward to a place in a delegation as a reward for dedicated service. Being chosen as a delegate is often a mixed reward, though, as delegates must pay for their own way to and from the convention as well as for accommodations while there.

In 1984, about 5,200 delegates and alternates will attend the Democratic convention in San Francisco, down slightly from the 5,400 who attended in 1980. Republicans will send 2,234 representatives and a like number of alternates to Dallas.

In apportioning delegate votes to the states, the national parties have generally been guided by two considerations: the population of the state and the voting strength of the party in that state. Population has been recognized by factoring in the state electoral vote; party strength has been recognized by giving bonus delegates to states where the party did well in recent elections.

The Ripon Society, an organization of Republican liberals, challenged their party's 1976 bonus system by arguing that it discriminates against larger states by reducing their influence. Specifically, California, with nearly 10 percent of the nation's population, got only 7.5 percent of the 1976 Republican convention delegates, and New York, with 9 percent of the population, got only 6.8 percent of the delegate vote. The U.S. Court of Appeals for the District of Columbia upheld the old formula, saying that, under the First Amendment, political parties can manage their own affairs without interference from the courts.

Sometimes the choice of a nominee has already been effectively determined before the convention, as for instance in the case of an incumbent president. In that case the delegates play a ratifying role. If

no clear front-runner has emerged by the end of June, the delegates have a time of decision ahead of them during which preconvention party caucuses and special-interest gatherings take on new importance.

Before 1952, "brokered" conventions were common. Behind-the-scenes deals were often made, votes traded and a compromise candidate frequently chosen from the pack as the nominee. Since then, neither party has taken more than one ballot to choose a presidential nominee.

COMMITTEE WORK

Much of the preliminary work of the conventions is done by committees. There are four in the Republican party, focusing on credentials, resolutions (platform), rules and order of business, and permanent organization. The Democrats have three standing committees—platform, rules and credentials—and one special committee—arrangements—that administers the operations of the convention.

Democratic Party

The party's standing committees have 159 members with 156 votes. One hundred and thirty-one votes are allocated among states and territories by the same formula used to determine the size of national convention delegations; membership from each state or territory must be equally divided between men and women. Committee members are chosen by delegations to represent their presidential preferences proportionally. The remaining 25 members of each committee are chosen by the Executive Committee of the Democratic National Committee to represent party and elected officials and do not favor any presidential candidate. Members of the standing committees need not be delegates or alternates to the national convention. Meetings are open to the public.

The convention has final authority over decisions and recommendations of standing committees. The standing committees perform the following functions:

The *Platform Committee* prepares the party platform with the views of all presidential candidates taken into consideration. A minority report can reach the convention floor, but only if 25 percent of the committee members agree.

The *Rules Committee* recommends the permanent rules of the convention, the agenda, the permanent officers of the convention and

amendments to the charter of the party. It can offer resolutions on matters that do not fall under the purview of the other convention committees.

The *Credentials Committee* recommends to the convention the resolution of any challenges involving delegates chosen for the convention.

Republican Party

In 1984, the Republicans will retain their practice of having one man and one woman from each state delegation serve on each committee. Each state also gets one additional delegate representative to each committee. The District of Columbia, Puerto Rico, the Virgin Islands and Guam each are allotted one seat on each of the committees, as well. If a state delegation is too small for both a man and a woman to serve on all convention committees, then the delegation may allocate its appointments in any way it chooses.

The *Credentials Committee* receives and monitors credentials of all delegates and alternates and determines the permanent roll of the convention. If there is a challenge the Republican National Committee makes every effort to resolve it before the convention, although disputes may be brought to the floor.

The *Resolutions Committee* drafts the party platform for the next four years. Months before the convention begins, research is begun and preliminary work gets under way with subcommittees focusing on various issues.

The *Committee on Rules and Order of Business* drafts the rules to be adopted by the convention covering proceedings, organization of the national committee and attendance at the next convention.

The *Permanent Organization Committee* recommends a set of ongoing officers for the convention, the most important of whom is the permanent chair.

THE CONVENTION BEGINS

When a convention—Democratic or Republican—begins, the national chair soon yields the gavel to a temporary chair picked in advance by the national committee. He or she presides while housekeeping matters are taken care of and then yields to the permanent chair, who presides during the platform debates and the nominating activities. The permanent convention chair has traditionally been chosen ahead of the con-

vention by consultation among party leaders. The convention merely ratifies the choice after it is presented. Since fairness to all contending factions by the presiding officer is a must if the convention is not to be disrupted, persons of stature and moderation are chosen. Present and former Speakers of the House of Representatives are especially favored.

The first highlight of the national convention is the famous "keynote address," usually given by the temporary chair. Many up-and-coming young politicians have launched their careers by means of a rousing keynote speech.

Following the keynote, delegate credentials and convention rules are accepted. At this point, any credentials battles between slates of delegates will be brought before the convention for decision if neither the national committee nor the credentials committee has been able to iron out the dispute.

Next, the platform committee reads its report. The significance of the platform does not lie in the fact that it will bind the nominees to a program. What is important is that the planks indicate which faction will control the nomination, especially if great differences exist among the contenders. In 1980, for example, Republicans removed a plank that had been in the platform for years—support for the Equal Rights Amendment; it was a clear signal that the conservative philosophy would prevail. A platform may also serve a symbolic purpose by providing an occasion for debate that allows dissidents to vent their grievances. This then is the first step toward an important convention purpose: closing ranks behind the slate in order to win the general election.

NOMINATING THE PRESIDENT

While debates over housekeeping matters and the platform are going on, delegations will caucus and recaucus, presidential hopefuls and those empowered to speak for them will try to build their delegate strength, promises will be made and, perhaps, bargains struck.[2] With the final platform plank completed, attention will turn to the convention's chief purpose, the nomination of the presidential candidate.

The candidate's name is placed in nomination by a prominent supporter. The order of nominations is determined by lot for the Democrats. Republicans hold a roll call by state.

The nominating speech for each candidate is traditionally followed by a demonstration of support from backers plus a series of seconding

speeches. Again, because of the role of television and the desire to have the nominee speak before the largest possible audience, both parties now put limits on the nominating speeches and the demonstrations.

Both parties also have attempted to keep frivolous candidates from being nominated by requiring candidates to present evidence of substantial support before their names can be placed in nomination.

After the close of nominations, the roll of the states for the casting of votes is called. Dilatory actions of past conventions, such as lengthy speeches by a delegation chair when announcing the state's vote, or the polling of each member of the delegation, are discouraged. States may pass when their turn comes and then vote at the end of the roll call or they may switch their votes before the final tally is announced. These measures are sometimes used as tactical maneuvers for a favored candidate or as a way of jumping on the bandwagon of a winning candidate.

In both parties, a majority vote is now sufficient to nominate. If no candidate receives a majority on the first ballot, the roll is called again until someone does receive a majority. Previously, under the Democrats' unit rule, a majority of one in a delegation could swing the entire delegation's voting strength behind a particular candidate, but this is no longer permitted. Republicans never used a unit rule.

While the roll call of states edges along in a close ballot, millions of people all over the country mark convention tally sheets as they watch on television or listen to the radio. When a state delegation's vote finally carries a candidate past the tip point to victory, pandemonium breaks loose in the convention hall, often making it a difficult feat for the chair to finish calling the roll.

CHOOSING THE VICE-PRESIDENT

One more task faces the delegates before they can head for home, and that is to nominate a vice-presidential candidate. The official nomination, as in the case of the presidential candidate, is made by state roll call, but the procedure is admittedly less suspenseful. Traditionally, the wishes of the presidential nominee are honored in the choice of running mate. That choice is known to all by roll-call time so that the nomination is a formality only and is sometimes made by acclamation. Occasionally there is some grumbling from delegates and even a battle for the nomination, as in 1956 at the Democratic convention when presidential nominee Adlai Stevenson threw the vice-presidential nomination open to the convention.

The selection of a vice-presidential nominee has usually been largely a matter of balancing the election ticket for maximum vote-getting potential. So, southerner Jimmy Carter in 1976 chose liberal Minnesotan Walter Mondale and Californian Ronald Reagan picked his close rival, George Bush of Texas, for the second spot on the ticket in 1980.

The Constitution assigns the vice-president very few duties other than to succeed to the office of president if it becomes vacant or if the president becomes disabled and is unable to function as president. But the office, which rarely got much attention in the past, has become more important in recent years in the eyes of the electorate. Franklin Roosevelt's death while in office, Eisenhower's serious illnesses, Kennedy's assassination, Nixon's resignation and the attempt on Reagan's life all indicate that the individual chosen to fill the vice-president's role must be of presidential timber. Throughout his term of office, President Carter regularly assigned broad responsibilities to Vice-President Mondale and kept him informed on a daily basis—in marked contrast to the treatment of previous vice-presidents. And President Reagan has given Vice-President Bush a major role as spokesperson for his administration.

Leaders in both parties have looked thoughtfully at the process of vice-presidential selection, questioning the haste sometimes shown in choosing a president's running mate. Many critics object to the fact that the victorious presidential nominee does the choosing, leaving delegates no role except to endorse. Criticism does not end there. Others have continued to question the role of the vice-president, with Arthur Schlesinger, Jr., calling for abolition of the office, and others proposing multiple vice-presidents to share the work of administering the executive branch.

THE ACCEPTANCE SPEECH

The final big moment for the convention is the acceptance speech by the presidential nominee. This custom is comparatively new. Before 1932, candidates did not go to conventions. Rather, delegations were sent to inform the winners of their nominations. In 1932, Franklin D. Roosevelt broke that tradition and flew to Chicago to accept the nomination personally, and all candidates have done so since. Although candidates usually do not begin formal campaigning until Labor Day, the acceptance speech sets the tone for the coming election. For example, in 1964, when Barry Goldwater proclaimed that "extremism in the

defense of liberty is no vice," he was signaling that he did not intend to moderate his conservative views during the coming campaign.

TELEVISION AT THE NATIONAL CONVENTIONS

Along with party reforms, radio and television have removed much of the secret, "smoke-filled-room" atmosphere from the national conventions. Television, especially, with its live coverage of events in and around the convention hall and convention city, has brought the proceedings into millions of homes.

As a result, there are often more media representatives at the convention than there are delegates, a situation that many critics call a case of the tail wagging the dog. They complain that the television networks often cut away from convention proceedings (such as seconding speeches) to present their own interviews, profiles and special reports. Nevertheless, both parties take care to schedule their most important events at a time when television viewing is likely to be at its peak. It may be inconvenient for politicians to trip over TV cables and hide from cameras, but full convention coverage has come to be expected by American voters. The careful viewer is likely to know as much as or more than the delegates themselves about what is going on at the convention. Like the football watcher, the stay-at-home participant has the advantage of the instant replay and the behind-the-scenes interview. Undoubtedly, more Americans are aware of how a presidential candidate is nominated than ever before, thanks to television.

☆ 8 ☆

THE GENERAL ELECTION CAMPAIGN

Traditionally, candidates have spent the time between their nominations and Labor Day—the calm eye of the campaign hurricane—resting, planning strategy for the upcoming two campaign months and making last-minute staff changes. Which political bases to touch, how to spread financial resources, where to raise more money, how best to use the media, how to make use of celebrity endorsements and how to motivate and organize local or state party workers are all decisions that must be reaffirmed before the final push.

At this point, too, candidates and voters alike have become weary, having gone through many months of increasing political activity. The print and broadcast media have been saturated with political advertising, analysis and campaign news since before the primary season began. Now, new enthusiasm must be generated for the crucial general election campaign.

Nominees must unite their parties and reorganize and supplement their staffs by recruiting from the ranks of their defeated rivals. They must strive to keep damaging or embarrassing incidents to a minimum while trying to win over the undecided, apathetic or hostile voters who can decide a close election. All this is prelude to the presidential campaign, a time when the nation seems to pause, reexamine its needs and goals and, with the alternatives narrowed down, prepare to select a leader.

CAMPAIGN ORGANIZATION

The principal purpose of a presidential campaign is to win votes by appealing to as many kinds of people as possible in as many different ways as possible. To do this with a potential electorate of more than 170 million people is a staggering task that demands good organization, a large staff and a great deal of money. The day of the "front-porch campaign" is over. In 1860 Abraham Lincoln won the election for the Republican party without leaving Springfield, Illinois, or making a single speech. One hundred years later, Republican nominee Richard Nixon traveled 65,000 miles, made 212 speeches, visited all 50 states—and lost.

Since Eisenhower entered politics in 1952, presidential candidates have created national organizations, independent of the national and state party organizations, to run their campaigns. The FECA has made the establishment of such committees mandatory for handling campaign contributions and expenditures. As campaigns have grown more complex, campaign organizations have become more professional, relying on political consultants, media experts and pollsters to provide information and advice. A close watch is kept on the nation's mood and the opponent's progress, so that strategy and tactics can be quickly altered to meet changing circumstances.

Campaign organizations vary in structure. However, most include a director and manager at the national level who supervise the work of numerous specialists, such as schedulers, public relations experts, issue advisors and speech writers. Campaign staffs keep in close touch with special interest groups such as minorities, unions or small business owners. A field coordinator maintains contact with state campaign and party committees. The treasurer keeps financial records and sees that FEC reports are filed.

Campaign organizations work with the media watching their every move. Dissension and confusion in the ranks are quickly reported, with the implication drawn that a candidate who cannot run a campaign organization will not be able to run the country. Reporters also watch the campaign funding process.

As party regulars have had less to say in the selection of the party's standard bearer, candidates have become increasingly independent. Reagan in 1980 and Carter in 1976 ran as party "outsiders" and tended to rely on their own primary campaign staffs from California and Georgia respectively. The parties, however, do provide volunteer help, contacts, get-out-the-vote and registration drives, campaign parapher-

nalia like buttons and bumper stickers, opinion research, publicity and other resources, including contributions of funds as permitted under the FECA. The successful campaign committee will also find a way to tap volunteer resources while ensuring that the presidential nominee and the nominee's campaign manager retain overall control.

The state and local party organizations, from central committee to precinct level, play an important role in the campaign. They keep up enthusiasm at the grass roots, distribute campaign literature and provide staff for headquarters and polling places. Good advance work and cooperation with state and local party volunteers and elected officials are important to make a campaign tour effective. The organization at the local level also keeps national headquarters informed about which bases must be touched and which fences need mending.

There are two kinds of volunteer groups in a presidential campaign. First are the party-affiliated groups such as Young Democrats or Young Republicans, State Federation of Republican or Democratic Women, and local or district Democratic or Republican clubs. These groups are organizationally separate from the parties but work closely with them. A second type is the "Citizens for John Doe Club." Such groups spring to life in every presidential campaign and are kept organizationally distinct for several reasons. They provide a way for volunteers to work for the national ticket without working for all party candidates, and they also may provide a special way to appeal to specific groups such as ethnic minorities or professional organizations. In 1960, for example, some 200 local-level Viva Kennedy clubs were organized in the 21 states with high concentrations of Spanish-speaking citizens.

Both parties also receive help in the form of money and volunteers from the major interest groups such as labor, business and agriculture. (See Chapter 5 regarding the activities of corporate and union political action committees and the role that independent expenditures can play.) No party can depend upon undivided support from any interest group, however; labor unions, for example, have long been a prime source of support for the Democratic party, but their efforts were divided in 1980 when many rank-and-file union members overrode their national leadership to work and vote for Ronald Reagan. The business community, often thought of as being pro-Republican, also makes contributions to the Democrats.

CAMPAIGN STRATEGY

ampaign strategy is an overall plan to use the available resources and
e strengths of the candidate to the best advantage to win the requisite
mber of electoral votes to be elected president of the United States. It
developed from lessons learned in the successful campaign for the
omination and the expertise of the pollsters, analysts and consultants
orking with the campaign organization.

Campaign strategy is influenced by many factors—the role of the
edia, the mood of the country, the economic climate and even events
erseas. It must be constantly revised and refocused to keep pace with
anging conditions. For example, the presidential campaign in 1980
as greatly affected by the Iranian hostage crisis that was taking place at
e same time. In 1984 the state of the economy and foreign policy are
re to be important issues.

New campaign finance rules have a profound effect on strategy. One
' the first major decisions a campaign organization must make is
hether to accept federal funds and the accompanying limitations on
mpaign contributions and expenditures, or to operate with private
ancing. Recently, candidates have chosen to take advantage of the
deral funding option and leave supplementary fund raising to the
gular party organization and independent committees.

The work begun during the convention—uniting the party behind a
gle candidate after what may have been a bitter fight for the nomina-
n—must continue. This effort and the drive to mobilize supporters
d capture the electoral votes of key states determine campaign travel
ans and scheduling. Candidates concentrate efforts on swing states,
ile making token appearances in states where they are assured of
tory and conceding those states where they have little chance to win.
is planning is done against a background of party officials clamoring
r an appearance by the standard-bearer in their states to motivate party
rkers, increase interest and turnout, and boost the campaigns of the
rty's contenders for state and local offices. It is also planned within
e framework of limited financial resources, time and the candidate's
mina.

Candidates must determine the image they wish to project and how
st to bring their message to as many potential voters as possible,
owing that voters base their decisions on the candidate's party, stand
issues and leadership qualities. They must decide how to appeal to
factions within their own parties while also attracting independents

and dissatisfied voters from other parties. Democratic candidates start with a larger party base (see Chapter 3) and can make a more partisan appeal, while Republicans must appeal to a broader range of the electorate. Incumbent contenders often choose to appear "presidential," and seek to be portrayed as too busy with important official duties to take to the campaign trail.

On issues, candidates can either appeal to a broad coalition of voters by blurring their stands on controversial issues or try to appeal to special interests by taking a bold and forthright stand. Often this decision has already been made by the selection of a nominee from either the broad mainstream of the party or the more extreme margins.

During the nominating process it is crucial for candidates to mobilize early support from a squadron of devoted workers and the voters who turn out for primaries and caucuses. Thus, candidates are motivated to take strong stands in order to appeal to a dedicated group of zealous supporters in the initial stages of their campaigns. But they must also allow for flexibility later on, when they need to appeal to a broader electorate, without appearing to renege on earlier commitments.

Political writer Richard Reeves suggests that the most successful politician may be the candidate who creates no enemies—the lowest common denominator.[1] And Alex Armedaris, president of a campaign management firm, advises candidates to sound as if they are saying something but actually to say nothing: "A strong position on an issue will only turn voters off." However, in recent years, a more aggressive press and the voters themselves have appeared to demand that candidates take more definite stands on the issues.

Projecting a presidential "image" has become increasingly important as more voters receive their information and impressions from television. Candidates seek to appear decisive, competent and assertive, and television ads have been turned to as the best way for the campaign organization to present its candidate as they want him or her to be perceived. An important strategic decision is how much television and other advertising will be used, as well as when and where to target it. Because media advertising is so expensive, it must be distributed carefully throughout the campaign period so momentum is built early and sustained and then followed by a media blitz just before the election.

CAMPAIGN TACTICS

While campaign strategy looks at the big picture, campaign tactics govern the day-to-day activities that implement the strategy. Even more than strategy, tactics must be flexible and able to be changed quickly as events warrant. Whereas strategy is developed and controlled from the national campaign headquarters, tactical considerations often determine the actions of the national and state party organizations, state and local campaign offices and volunteer and independent committees.

Successful tactics include careful advance work that guarantees a full house at a campaign appearance, or frequent "media opportunities" that show the candidate acting "presidential" or interacting with citizens who belong to important minority or ethnic groups. Methods of bringing the candidate's message and image before the voters range from leaflets passed out or distributed door-to-door by volunteers to nationwide television ads. Celebrity endorsements and special appearances have become an important feature of campaigns.

Even if the candidate's campaign committee is not soliciting contributions, the party and independent committees are doing so, using traditional techniques like fund raisers and new tactics like sophisticated, computerized direct mail appeals. At the same time, such committees are deciding how best to help their candidate through advertising, financing opinion polls, setting up telephone banks to identify supporters or recruiting volunteers.

Tactical decisions also may govern how time, money, paid and volunteer staff and the candidate's energy will be allocated. This involves targeting—expanding effort where it will be most effective rather than trying to cover all areas and groups. Opinion polling can reveal those who are already in the candidate's corner and those who could not be won over by any action, thus helping campaigns target their resources. They can show where extra advertising would be useful.

Because the last two national elections have shown that women are now voting in greater proportions and that they tend to vote on the basis of issue stands that often differ from those of men, targeting will no doubt be directed toward women in the 1984 presidential campaign. Political advisers and leaders of women's groups point out that the majority of voters now are women, a factor that candidates cannot ignore. Other groups, such as blacks, Hispanics and older citizens are beginning to capitalize on the importance of voting to achieve their ends.

As the campaign draws to a close, the last step is to translate support into votes. Last-minute television appeals, phone calls from volunteers and door-to-door canvassing are used to urge registered voters to go to the polls. Campaign workers offer rides and baby-sitting and hand out leaflets outside the polling places. In the final analysis, the success of a campaign effort is measured very simply: by victory or defeat.

MASS MEDIA IN CAMPAIGNING

Although some voters learn about candidates through direct mail, word of mouth or leaflets left at their door, most information on presidential candidates comes through the mass media—television, radio, news-papers and magazines. The way the media cover the campaign and the way the candidates use paid media advertising can make a vital difference in election results.

News Coverage and Equal-Time Provisions

For the national news media, covering a presidential campaign has taken on the proportions of conducting a major military campaign. The logistics alone present a significant organizational challenge. Campaign stories often begin as long as two years before the election. Today's media organizations have the ability to determine the shape and substance of a campaign—the ability to mold images, to define issues, to play up some candidates and play down others, to interpret polls and the results of primaries, to generate a sense of gathering momentum or impending defeat.

Given this potential power, journalists must make some key decisions. How much coverage should each candidate receive? Should coverage focus on what the candidates say in official position papers? Should reporters cover details of what candidates actually do in a day of campaigning or their records in office? Should reporters attempt to make analytical interpretations of candidates' views and personalities?

The colorfulness of campaign reporting ebbs and flows, depending on the nature of the candidates, the events of a campaign and reporters' predictions. In 1960, Theodore White put his imprint on political reporting with his chronicle of the Kennedy/Nixon race in *Making of the President 1960*. In a reporting classic, he laid out a bird's-eye view of what political campaigning was all about—excitement and drama wrapped around a hectic scramble for the "grand prize."

Since then, in-depth reporting has examined candidates' personalities and life styles, scrutinized family life and watched campaign organizations for signs of trouble or changes in direction. However, some within the media industry feel that attention to such matters obscures serious coverage of the candidates' stands on issues and their qualifications for office. Recently television reporters and print journalists have taken a harder stand with candidates by pressing them to answer tough questions.

Of all the media, television bears the greatest responsibilities in campaign coverage, for it is the major source of political news for most voters. Yet there are many obstacles to thorough television coverage of campaign issues. Straightforward discussion of issues does not produce much color or excitement for TV cameras; the medium thrives on action. The short time available for the evening news further restricts any real analysis of issues, and TV costs play a large part in curbing ideal coverage. However, news shows have begun to devote more time to candidate profiles, although critics complain that they still tend to be superficial. Interview shows, such as the *McNeil-Lehrer Newshour,* feature in-depth questioning of the candidates.

EQUAL-TIME PROVISIONS

The so-called equal-time rule (Section 315) of the Federal Communications Act requires a broadcaster who sells or gives time to a candidate to make available equal opportunities to all competing candidates for the same office, including minor-party and independent candidates. In the past, this rule has effectively discouraged coverage of major candidates by some broadcasters who did not want to include minor candidates in their broadcasts. Exceptions to the rule may occur when a candidate is shown in a bona fide newscast, interview or news documentary (where the candidate's appearance is only incidental to the subject of the documentary), or in on-the-spot coverage of a bona fide news event. The Federal Communications Commission has ruled that candidate debates and forums as bona-fide news events are exempt from equal-opportunities (equal-time) provisions. The LWVEF-sponsored Presidential Forums and Debates were broadcast under the news event exemption.

In 1976, a series of televised forums, in which voters and experts questioned the major presidential candidates, was sponsored by the League of Women Voters Education Fund (LWVEF) in cooperation with the Public Broadcasting Service. The forums were scheduled just before the major primaries and provided for in-depth consideration of one major issue area for each program. And after the party conventions, the LWVEF sponsored four debates—three between presidential candidates Ford and Carter and one between vice-presidential candidates Mondale and Dole—which were covered by the networks. To sharpen the discussion, experienced reporters and issue experts quizzed the candidates.

The 1980 presidential debates, also sponsored by the LWVEF, started with a field of seven Republican contenders who took part in a forum in February, at the very beginning of the delegate selection period. By the time the second forum was held in March, the field had been reduced to four contenders. Finally, by the end of April only two Republican hopefuls were still in the race—Ronald Reagan and George Bush.

As the summer progressed and after the nominations of Reagan and Carter, John Anderson made a strong nationwide showing as a declared independent candidate, and he wished to be included in any presidential debates. The LWVEF Board of Trustees had set criteria for participation in three planned encounters during the fall general election campaign. Only two debates were actually held. Anderson and Reagan debated on September 21 in Baltimore, Maryland. Carter declined to participate. However, Carter and Reagan did debate on October 28 in Cleveland, Ohio. Since this was the only face-to-face meeting of the two major party candidates, it took on added importance for the candidates as well as for the public.

As the 1984 campaign got under way, the League of Women Voters Education Fund again announced that it would sponsor both primary and general election debates among presidential contenders.

The Print Media

While television has a greater capability than print to capture a large audience, news coverage would be incomplete without the wire services, daily newspapers and news weeklies. The print media can probe the personalities of candidates and offer extensive serialized treatises on every aspect of a campaign in a way television and radio are not

Republican presidential contenders debate the issues during the preconvention season in 1980. Left to right are Phillip Crane, George Bush, moderator Howard K. Smith, Ronald Reagan and John Anderson.

equipped to do. Not being subject to the technical constraints of the broadcasting trade, journalists in the print media have a greater opportunity to fully develop coverage, no matter how many candidates are out on the campaign trail.

The national wire services—Associated Press (AP) and United Press International (UPI)—provide the most widely circulated stories in the country. And what the wire reporters view as the "lead" of a story will often end up as the meat of the story in a thousand daily newspapers across the country. Because of tight deadlines and space limitations, however, these stories are generally not as analytical as the syndicated byline articles sent out by the *Los Angeles Times, Washington Post* and *New York Times.*

Use of Radio and TV Advertising by Candidates

Candidates have come to rely extensively on the broadcast media to appeal for votes. Through short TV and radio spots or elaborately prepared TV feature programs produced by their own media specialists

and lasting 15 minutes to an hour, candidates hope to accentuate their own qualities and downgrade those of their opponents. Spot commercials are useful in projecting a vivid, dynamic image and are not usually intended to convey much information, though they sometimes deal with issues.

The importance of radio and television is that they give the candidates massive, national exposure. Expensive though that exposure is, it takes less energy than in-person appearances, makes it possible to use travel time more efficiently and opens up a much wider audience. Personal contact may mean more to voters, but such contact becomes impractical when there is a whole nation to reach in a short time. TV and radio ads can be replayed again and again, maximizing their usefulness.

Use of television or radio spots peaks at the height of the campaign, usually just before election time. Many thoughtful persons fear that campaigns have become battles between advertising agencies rather than tests of candidates and issues. If much of a presidential campaign is stage-managed, they argue, voters will never see the "real" candidate or hear discussion of the "real" issues.

Television campaigning takes on an even greater significance to some critics when seen in the light of polling technology. Political advertising is increasingly based on survey research. Voters are polled as to what issues trouble them, what their attitudes are on certain issues and how they respond to candidates. This material is then used to design a campaign that will appeal to voters' special interests or even exploit their fears.

Media specialists defend their work on a number of grounds. They contend, on one hand, that television is overrated, that it is only one campaign tool. On the other hand, they say that even if it is influential, political advertising serves the same purpose as commercial advertising—to inform viewers of the products available. And even short spots can be produced in such a way that they give straightforward information on a candidate's position. Viewers know that the information is biased in favor of the product and make the necessary adjustments in their thinking. Skeptics doubt this rationale, feeling that voters do not have enough defenses against the soft sell and that, in any case, the media specialists are skillfully working to stay ahead of whatever defenses viewers have. Occasionally, the professionals are candid about the business they're in. Says one media specialist: "Damned right we don't explain. We don't educate, we motivate. That's our job. We're not teachers, we're political managers. We're trying to win."

☆ 9 ☆

THE
ELECTION

THE ELECTORAL COLLEGE SYSTEM

The actual mechanism of electing the president and the vice-president of the United States is a rather complicated process. The electoral college is one of the many compromises written into the Constitution of 1787. The founding fathers devised the electoral college to elect the president but they did not anticipate the emergence of national political parties or of a communications network able to bring presidential candidates before the entire electorate.

Providing that the president be chosen indirectly through the "electoral college" rather than directly by the voters in November was one of the founders' hedges against "popular passion." In the beginning, the electors had very real powers to work their will. Now, their sole function is to confirm a decision made by the electorate six weeks earlier.[1]

Under the Constitution, each state is authorized to choose electors for president and vice-president, the number always being the same as the combined number of U.S. senators and representatives allotted to that state. With 100 senators and 435 representatives in the United States, plus three electors for the District of Columbia provided by the Twenty-Third Amendment, the total electoral college vote is 538.[2]

Makeup and operation of the electoral college itself are tightly defined by the Constitution, but the method of choosing electors is left to the states. In the beginning many states did not provide for popular election of the presidential electors. Today, however, electors are chosen by direct popular vote in every state. When voters vote for president, they are actually voting for the electors pledged to their presidential candidate. (Electors are named by state party organizations. Serving as an elector is considered an honor, a reward for faithful service.)

With the political parties in control of presidential politics, the function of the electoral college has changed drastically. Rather than having individuals seek to become electors and then vote for whomever they please for president, the parties have turned the process upside down by arranging slates of electors, all pledged to support the candidate nominated by the party.

In the earliest days of the electoral college, quite the opposite was true. Electors cast their votes for individual candidates rather than for party slates, with the majority winner being elected president and the runner-up, vice-president. This made for some bizarre situations, as in 1796 when the Federalist John Adams, with 71 votes, became president and the Democratic-Republican Thomas Jefferson, with 68, vice-president—roughly equivalent in modern times to an election in which Reagan and Carter would end up as president and vice-president. Then in 1800 Jefferson and his running mate, Aaron Burr, each won an identical number of electoral votes, forcing the election into the House of Representatives, which resolved it in Jefferson's favor. It was to avoid any similar occurrence that the Twelfth Amendment was passed in 1804. This required the electors to cast two separate ballots, one for president and the other for vice-president. It has been the only constitutional change made in the electoral college system, other than to add three electoral votes for the District of Columbia in 1961.

Presidential and vice-presidential candidates of a party run as a team. In most of the states, it is the names of the candidates rather than the names of the electors that appear on the ballot; in the other states, both candidates and electors are identified. The victor in each state is determined by counting the votes for each slate of electors; the slate receiving the most votes (the plurality, not necessarily the majority of the votes cast) is declared the winner.

To be elected to the presidency a candidate must receive an absolute majority (270) of the electoral votes cast. If no candidate receives a majority, the House of Representatives picks the winner from the top

three, with each state delegation in the House casting only one vote, regardless of its size. Only two U.S. elections have been decided this way (1800 and 1824).

The vice-president is elected at the same time by the same indirect, winner-take-all method that chooses the president, but the electors vote separately for the two offices. If no vice-presidential candidate receives a majority, the Senate picks the winner from the top two, each senator voting as an individual. The Senate has not made the choice since 1836.

The Electoral College Pro and Con

The electoral college mechanism has not lacked for critics over the years. The basic objection is that the system clearly has the potential to frustrate the popular will in the selection of a president and a vice-president. Because of the aggregation of electoral votes by state, it is possible that a candidate might win the most popular votes but lose in the electoral college voting. This happened in 1824 (when the election was thrown into the House, in 1876 (when there were disputed electors from several states) and in 1888. The winner-take-all system means literally that the candidate team that wins *most* of the popular votes (the plurality vote winner) in a particular state gets *all* of the electoral votes in that state, and the loser gets none, even if the loss is by a slim popular-vote margin. Thus a candidate who fails to carry a particular state receives not a single *electoral* vote in that state for the *popular* votes received. Since presidential elections are won by electoral—not popular—votes, it is the electoral vote tally that election-night viewers watch for and that tells the tale.

Another problem cited by critics is the possibility of "faithless electors" who defect from the candidate to whom they are pledged.

Most recently, in 1976, a Republican elector in the state of Washington cast his vote for Ronald Reagan instead of Gerald Ford, the Republican presidential candidate. Earlier in 1972, a Republican elector in Virginia deserted Nixon to vote for the Libertarian party candidate. And in 1968, Nixon lost another Virginia elector, who bolted to George Wallace.

The main danger of "faithless electors" is that the candidate who wins the popular vote could wind up one or two votes short of a majority in the electoral college and could lose the election on a technicality. This prospect becomes more probable when there are third-party or

independent candidates who could negotiate with electors before they vote.

Many see the apportioning of the electoral college votes by states as a basic flaw, because it gives each of the smaller states at least three electoral votes, even though on a straight population basis some might be entitled to only one or two.

Critics of the system also argue that the possibility that an election could be thrown into the House of Representatives is undemocratic, since for such a decision each state has a single vote, a fact that gives the sparsely populated or small state equal weight with more populous states such as California or New York. The two occasions when it occurred (1800 and 1824) were marked by charges of "deals" and "corrupt bargains." In any event, giving each state one vote in the House of Representatives regardless of the number of people represented is not consistent with the widely accepted concept of one person one vote. Also one vote per state in the House of Representatives may not necessarily result in a choice that replicates the electoral vote winner in that state in November.

Those who argue in favor of retaining the present system state that there is too much uncertainty over whether any other method would be an improvement. They point out that many of the complaints about the electoral college apply just as well to the Senate and, to some extent, to the House. They fear that reform could lead to the dismantling of the federal system.

Another argument made by defenders of the electoral college is that the present method serves American democracy well by fostering a two-party system and thwarting the rise of splinter parties that have plagued many European democracies. The winner-take-all system means that minor parties get few electoral votes and that a president who is the choice of the nation as a whole emerges. In the present system, splinter groups could not easily throw an election into the House. Supporters feel strongly that if the electors fail to agree on a majority president, it is in keeping with the federal system that the House of Representatives, *voting as states,* makes the selection.

Supporters also argue that the electoral college system democratically reflects population centers by giving urban areas electoral power; that is where the most votes are. Thus together, urban states come close to marshalling the requisite number of electoral votes to elect a president.

A final argument is that for the most part, the electoral college system has worked. No election in this century has been decided in the House

of Representatives.[3] Further, the winner's margin of votes is usually enhanced in the electoral vote—a mathematical happening that can make the winner in a divisive and close election seem to have won more popular support than he actually did. This is thought to aid the healing of election scars and help the new president in governing.

Proposals for Change

Discontent with the system was stimulated in the 1960s by the Wallace third-party movement and in 1980 by John Anderson's initially strong showing as an independent candidate with nationwide appeal. Also, the Supreme Court's one-person-one-vote ruling on legislative districts underscored the importance of equitable distribution of votes. A number of proposals for altering the way the president and the vice-president are elected have been made. Most would require constitutional amendment, though states can on their own change their state laws governing the way they choose electors.

One set of proposals looks toward keeping the electoral college but eliminating its winner-take-all features. This shift could be brought about by choosing most electors on a congressional district basis, with only two electors per state chosen statewide. A 1969 Maine law provides for this method, and similar legislation has been considered in several other states. Alternatively, the office of elector could be eliminated and the electoral votes of a state simply assigned to candidates on the basis of the popular vote each received. Constitutional amendments to that effect have been introduced in Congress but none has passed. These changes might eliminate some distortion of the popular vote, but they would not answer the complaint that the people do not elect the president directly.

Former Sen. Birch Bayh repeatedly introduced a constitutional amendment providing for direct election of the president and the vice-president. Under the Bayh plan, candidates for president and vice-president would be required to run together in each state and the District of Columbia, and voters would make their choices directly, without any intervening slate of electors. If the candidate team with the most votes received at least 40 percent of the nationwide popular vote, that pair would be declared elected; if no pair received that amount there would be a runoff election between the two top pairs.

Direct election of the president along the lines of the Bayh plan would effectively bring the one-person-one-vote principle to presidential elec-

tions. Its advocates claim that direct election would help the two-party system. Any dangers to the federal system, they argue, would be more than outweighed by the right of all the people of the United States to choose their two top elected officials directly. Opponents of direct election hold that this particular plan for change might necessitate the holding of two elections because of the runoff provision, thus making the presidential election process even more costly and drawn out than it is already. Following the defeat of the proposed amendment by the Senate in 1979, no further significant effort has been made to revive the plan.

ELECTION DAY

A presidential election day is the consummation of the study, the planning and training, the grueling work and travel, the meeting and talking, the writing and speech making, the persuading and financing, that have been done on behalf of and by the presidential candidates. It is their day of victory or of defeat.

For many hundreds of other people, it is a long, hard day that starts for some at five in the morning when precinct workers, organized to catch voters before they leave for work, nail VOTE signs along the streets and slip reminder sheets under the doors of "their voters." In some places, the polls open at 6:00 A.M., and a full complement of poll workers, officials, watchers and policemen must be on hand. Dozens of kinds of tasks, painstakingly planned, have been assigned to volunteers and regular party workers of all ages and talents. Party poll watchers, message runners, drivers to take voters to the polls, teen-agers to electioneer, people to babysit, party workers to telephone registered voters who have not appeared at the polls, Scouts to give out "I have voted" tags—all swing into action for a long, tiring, exciting day.

Voting is supervised by election officials representing both major parties. These officials are paid a nominal fee by the local election office. Their work begins before the polls open and is far from over when the polls close. They are trained and responsible for ensuring proper voting procedures and for generally overseeing the conduct of the election in the polling places. They may accept absentee ballots and supervise the process of assisting voters whose physical disabilities entitle them to receive help in the voting booth. They count the votes and report the returns to the central election office, or in the case of punchcard ballots, process them in the precinct or take them to a central computer counting center.

For the candidates, election day is like an opening night for a Broadway producer. Everything that can be done has been done or is being done by campaign workers. By tradition, candidates do not campaign on election day or even make public appearances other than to vote at their own polling places. As the day ends and the time for the polls to close approaches, each candidate, like millions of other Americans, settles in front of the television set and waits for the election results to come in.

Reporting the Results

At one time, election nights in America were important social events. Friends and neighbors gathered at the local store or in private homes and entertained one another with food, drink, and conversation as the election results trickled in over telegraph wire or radio station. Spokespersons for candidates who were trailing in the early returns talked bravely of trends that had not yet developed and reminded supporters to "wait for the downstate returns." The leading candidates said cautiously that it was "too early to tell yet" and continued to make gloomy predictions until it was time to claim victory and congratulate the opposition on a "clean campaign." The vigil often went on until dawn.

Modern television and advances in election technology have considerably shortened the suspense period. The national networks now begin coverage of election returns before the polls close and continue until the result is known—a result that is not usually long in coming. At one time poll workers carefully counted paper ballots, inscribed the results on official sheets and transported the ballot box to the county seat where officials would finally give the results to the media. Today, paper ballots are rare outside rural areas, and voting machines or punchcard ballots eliminate time-consuming ballot counting. Once the polls have closed, election officials simply compile results from voting machine printer sheets or from computer tabulation of punchcard ballots. Nor do the media wait for the results to be officially reported. They hire precinct watchers to get the results at the same time election officials do and report them to the networks over special telephone lines. In that way, the television networks can flash some results on the screen soon after the polls have closed.

Television not only reports results that have been tabulated, it also projects winners on the basis of a very few returns or from "exit interviews." The procedure is the same one often used by politicians in a less extensive and less scientific way. Projections from "key" pre-

cincts—those whose returns usually closely parallel the complete returns for the state in question—are identified beforehand and information about them is fed into computers. When returns come in, the computer is programmed to compare them with the returns of other years from the same precinct and project who the eventual winner in the state will be. If the information originally stored in the computer was incomplete or inaccurate, the predictions will, of course, be wrong. From these projections, the modern viewer often is told who has carried a state 30 minutes after the polls have closed, even though less than 5 percent of the vote may have been tabulated. With projections from exit interviews, winners can be projected well before the polls close (see box "Early Projection of Election Results").

Very close elections cannot be called so quickly, and most of the network mistakes have come when the outcome was too hastily projected. On the whole, however, the projections have been accurate. There is no more "waiting for the downstate returns"; the computer has already taken such factors into account. In 1964, one network proclaimed Johnson the winner over Goldwater only a few hours after the first polls had closed. The 1968 and 1976 elections were much closer and winners were not projected until the morning after the election. The 1980 election winner, however, was announced by all networks and the defeated candidate had conceded before the polls had closed in the West.

In addition to reporting the results and projecting winners, the television networks also analyze the results and explain what has happened in demographic, social and economic terms. Scholars have done this for years, of course, but not on election night. Computers are used to marshal data enabling reporters to describe how the ethnic neighborhoods voted in Chicago, how a candidate is doing in farm areas, etc. The meaning of the election will be studied for years, but television, as usual, reports it first. In short, the viewer now knows as much about the outcome of the election before retiring on election night as it once took weeks to find out.

EARLY PROJECTION OF ELECTION RESULTS

Techniques such as exit polls and sample precinct analysis combined with modern computer technology have made possible the early projection of winners by networks and news services.

Following the 1980 election when Ronald Reagan was projected winner on all three networks before the polls closed in the West *and* when President Carter conceded the election at 9:45 P.M. EST, hearings were held in Congress to address the growing controversy over such practices. Critics charged that the networks' rush to project a winner overlooked the effect of early projections on voter turnout in the West and on close, nonpresidential races that could be affected by a less-than-expected turnout. Polls taken in the months following the 1980 election showed that many citizens in all parts of the country were angered and alarmed by the growing practice of predicting winners on the basis of exit polls (used only by NBC in 1980 but by ABC and CBS as well in the 1982 congressional elections) and sample precinct analysis.

Although all three networks announced in 1982 that they would voluntarily refrain from projecting election results in any state before the polls had closed in that state, none of them fully complied with that stated policy. Some legislators and network representatives alike have called for a variety of legislative proposals to remedy the situation, such as uniform poll closing time or 24-hour voting. But many fear such cures would be worse than the problem because of their effects on voting patterns or on the costs of administering elections. Others question what will happen if the media cease to simply report events but use techniques that might actually change the outcome of elections.

In spite of the problems caused by early projections in 1980, as of mid-1983, each of the national TV networks continued to maintain that their First Amendment rights would be abridged by any form of restraint on their ability to project winners.

THE FINAL STAGES

When the final election results are in, the entire country knows who the next president and vice-president will be, but the outcome must still be formalized. In December, the electors who were chosen in November travel to their respective state capitals for the brief ceremony of assembling to cast their official electoral votes, signing necessary documents and posing for pictures. Then they go home. Their brief moment of glory is soon over as state officials certify their results and transmit their official ballots to Washington. When Congress convenes in January, the electoral vote documents from all 50 states and the District of Columbia are opened before a joint session of the two houses and the official results announced. In nearly every American presidential election, this is a formality only. The election winner is already being referred to as the president-elect and has been preparing for weeks to assume office.

Presidential transitions are not easy for either the person leaving office or the person coming into it. A "lame duck" president must carry on with presidential duties even while carrying less weight than before the election in domestic, political and international circles. It is considered bad form for the president-elect to offer policy advice during the transitional period; an outgoing president does not usually seek it. The atmosphere of suspended animation that characterizes a presidential transition could probably cause some problems if a severe crisis should arise. For example, what should be the attitude of a president-elect should a nuclear confrontation with a foreign power develop in December? No one knows the answer because the country has been spared any such development, but the general attitude of presidents-elect has been that the country has only one president at a time, that the powers of the presidency do not come in stages but all at once. Today, an ordinary citizen; tomorrow, the most important elected official in the world.

At noon on January 20 following a presidential election, the term of the preceding president ends and that of the incoming president begins.[4] At a formal inauguration ceremony, the Chief Justice of the United States Supreme Court[5] swears in the president and the vice-president before members of Congress, government dignitaries, representatives of foreign governments and a host of important well-wishers. The new chief executive makes an inaugural address and a parade usually follows. A new president has begun the duties of office, the election process has concluded and a new election period now begins.

AFTERWORD

This book has been written to explain the presidential nomination and election process. Its premise is the value of individual participation at all stages of the operation.

The long and arduous path for "choosing the president" puts the presidential hopefuls up for scrutiny by giving you an opportunity to evaluate their performance: As *leaders*—their ability to inspire trust; as *administrators*—their organizational skills; and as *individuals*—their honesty, competence, sensitivity and integrity.

Their campaign organizations may be viewed as mini-White Houses —precursors of an administration-to-be. If you look closely you can see how they operate as money managers, how realistic their proposals are, how they deal with the press, how much personal contact they try to develop with the public, and how responsive they are to citizen concerns.

And you can do more than just watch. . . .

The thing to do is to start asking questions—find out who and where the party leaders are. Call your local party headquarters, volunteer your services, ask about times and places of meetings, ask your neighbors about what's what politically in your area, call the League of Women Voters. The qualification necessary for political involvement is interest.

You *can* make a difference.

No presidential election has ever been, or is likely to be, decided by

one vote, but it is true that more than once a shift of relatively few votes in the right states would have changed the outcome under the electoral college system. The most drastic case in recent years was the 1960 election—when John Kennedy won the presidential election by an average of only one vote per precinct.

The closer the balance between the parties in a state, the more important is your single vote, and with a real two-party system throughout the country, the competition for each vote is growing in practically every state. Even if the election outcome seems almost a foregone conclusion, a vote cast in a losing cause is not a wasted vote. It can be politically worthwhile as a way to build or retain strength for the future. If, for instance, every southern Republican had stopped voting during the years of Democratic domination of the South, the modern Republican party could never have developed as it has in recent years.

The legitimacy of the chief executive's leadership is affected by who, to begin with, elects the president. And if only a small fraction of the public turns out to vote the individual into office, our democratic system will fall short of its potential for the people to realize their power. Changes in all aspects of our political system—some of which have been described in this book—mean that in 1984 American government rests far more than ever before in our history on individual participation, on *your* participation, at every stage in the election process.

APPENDIXES

APPENDIX A

PROVISIONS IN THE U.S. CONSTITUTION RELATING TO THE PRESIDENCY

United States Constitution

ARTICLE II—The President
Section 1. The executive Power shall be vested in a President of the United States of America. He shall hold his Office during the Term of four Years, and, together with the Vice-President, chosen for the same Term, be elected, as follows.

Each state shall appoint, in such Manner as the Legislature thereof may direct, a Number of Electors, equal to the whole Number of Senators and Representatives to which the State may be entitled in the Congress: but no Senator or Representative, or Person holding an Office of Trust or Profit under the United States, shall be appointed an Elector.

The Congress may determine the Time of choosing the Electors, and the Day on which they shall give their Votes; which Day shall be the same throughout the United States.

AMENDMENT XII—Presidential Electors

The Electors shall meet in their respective states and vote by ballot for President and Vice-President, one of whom, at least, shall not be an inhabitant of the same state with themselves; they shall name in their ballots the person voted for as President, and in distinct ballots the person voted for as Vice-President, and they shall make distinct lists of all persons voted for as President, and of all persons voted for as Vice-President, and of the number of votes for each, which lists they shall sign and certify, and transmit sealed to the seat of the government of the United States, directed to the President of the Senate;—the President of the Senate shall, in presence of the Senate and House of Representatives, open all the certificates and the votes shall then be counted;—The person having the greatest number of votes for President, shall be the President, if such number be a majority of the whole number of Electors appointed; and if no person have such majority, then from the persons having the highest numbers not exceeding three on the list of those voted for as President, the House of Representatives shall choose immediately, by ballot, the President. But in choosing the President, the votes shall be taken by states, the representation from each state having one vote; a quorum for this purpose shall consist of a member or members from two-thirds of the states, and a majority of all the states shall be necessary to a choice. And if the House of Representatives shall not choose a President whenever the right of choice shall devolve upon them, before the fourth day of March[1] next following, then the Vice-President shall act as President, as in the case of the death or other constitutional disability of the President.[2]—The person having the greatest number of votes as Vice-President, shall be the Vice-President, if such number be a majority of the whole number of Electors appointed, and if no person have a majority, then from the two highest numbers on the list, the Senate shall choose the Vice-President; a quorum for the purpose shall consist of two-thirds of the whole number of Senators, and a majority of the whole number shall be necessary to a choice. But no person constitutionally ineligible to the office of President shall be eligible to that of Vice-President of the United States. (Ratified in 1804)

AMENDMENT XX—Lame-Duck Amendment

Section 3. If, at the time fixed for the beginning of the term of the President, the President elect shall have died, the Vice President elect shall become President. If a President shall not have been chosen before

the time fixed for the beginning of his term, or if the President elect shall have failed to qualify, then the Vice President elect shall act as President until a President shall have qualified; and the Congress may by law provide for the case wherein neither a President elect nor a Vice President elect shall have qualified, declaring who shall then act as President, or the manner in which one who is to act shall be selected, and such person shall act accordingly until a President or Vice President shall have qualified.

Section 4. The Congress may by law provide for the case of the death of any of the persons from whom the House of Representatives may choose a President whenever the right of choice shall have devolved upon them, and for the case of the death of any of the persons from whom the Senate may choose a Vice President whenever the right of choice shall have devolved upon them. (Ratified in 1933)

Proposed D.C. Representation Amendment
(sent to states for ratification in August 1979)

Section 1. For the purposes of representation in Congress, election of the President and Vice-President, and Article V of the Constitution, the District constituting the seat of government of the United States shall be treated as though it were a State.

Section 2. The exercise of the rights and powers conferred under this article shall be by the people of the District constituting the seat of government, and as shall be provided by the Congress.

Section 3. The twenty-third article of amendment to the Constitution of the United States is hereby repealed.

Section 4. This article shall be inoperative, unless it shall have been ratified as an amendment to the Constitution by the legislatures of three-fourths of the several States within seven years from the date of its submission.

APPENDIX B

THE PRESIDENTIAL OFFICE

Qualifications for Office

Natural-born citizen; at least 35 years old; 14 years or more a resident within the United States.

U.S. CONSTITUTION, ARTICLE II

Section 1. No person except a natural born citizen, or a Citizen of the United States, at the time of the Adoption of this Constitution, shall be eligible to the Office of President; neither shall any Person be eligible to that Office who shall not have attained to the Age of thirty-five Years, and been fourteen Years a Resident within the United States.

Term of Office

Four years, beginning on January 20 of the year following election.

U.S. CONSTITUTION, AMENDMENT XX

Section 1. The terms of the President and Vice President shall end at noon on the 20th day of January, and the terms of Senators and Representatives at noon on the 3d day of January, of the years in which such terms would have ended if this article had not been ratified; and the terms of their successors shall then begin.

No more than two terms or ten years.

U.S. CONSTITUTION, AMENDMENT XXII

No person shall be elected to the office of the President more than twice, and no person who has held the office of President, or acted as President, for more than two years of a term to which some other person was elected President shall be elected to the office of the President more than once. But this Article shall not apply to any person holding the office of President when this Article was proposed by the Congress, and shall not prevent any person who may be holding the office of President, or acting as President, during the term within which this Article becomes operative from holding the office of President or acting as President during the remainder of such term. (Ratified in 1951)

Presidential Oath of Office

U.S. CONSTITUTION, ARTICLE II

Section 1. Before he enter on the execution of his office, he shall take the following oath or affirmation: "I do solemnly swear (or affirm) that I will faithfully execute the Office of President of the United States, and will to the best of my Ability, preserve, protect and defend the Constitution of the United States."

Salary

President
$200,000 a year salary, taxable;
$50,000 a year expense allowance, taxable, to assist in defraying expenses resulting from official duties;
$100,000 a year, nontaxable, may be expended for travel expenses and official entertainment.

U.S. CONSTITUTION, ARTICLE II
Section 1. The President shall, at stated Times, receive for his Services, a Compensation, which shall neither be increased nor diminished during the period for which he shall have been elected, and he shall not receive within that Period any other Emolument from the United States, or any of them.

Ex-President
$66,000 a year lifetime pension, free mailing privileges, free office space;
Up to $90,000 a year for office help;
Secret Service protection for life;
$20,000 a year for widow.

Vice-President
$100,700 a year salary, taxable;
$10,000 a year, taxable, for expenses;
Use of official residence.

Duties and Powers of the President

U.S. CONSTITUTION, ARTICLE II
Section 2. (1) The President shall be Commander in Chief of the Army and Navy of the United States, and of the Militia of the several States, when called into the actual Service of the United States; he may require the Opinion in writing, of the principal Officer in each of the executive Departments, upon any subject relating to the Duties of their respective Offices, and he shall have Power to Grant Reprieves and Pardons for Offenses against the United States, except in Cases of Impeachment.
Section 2. (2) He shall have Power, by and with the Advice and Consent of the Senate, to make Treaties, provided two-thirds of the Senators present concur; and he shall nominate, and by and with the Advice and Consent of the Senate, shall appoint Ambassadors, other public Minis-

ters and Consuls, Judges of the supreme Court, and all other Officers of the United States, whose Appointments are not herein otherwise provided for, and which shall be established by Law: but the Congress may by Law vest the Appointment of such inferior officers, as they think proper, in the President alone, in the Courts of Law, or in the Heads of Departments.

Section 3. He shall from time to time give to the Congress Information of the State of the Union, and recommend to their Consideration such Measures as he shall judge necessary and expedient; he may, on extraordinary Occasions, convene both Houses, or either of them, and in Case of Disagreement between them, with Respect to the Time of Adjournment, he may adjourn them to such Time as he shall think proper; he shall receive Ambassadors and other public Ministers; he shall take Care that the Laws be faithfully executed, and shall Commission all the Officers of the United States.

Section 4. The President, Vice President, and all civil Officers of the United States, shall be removed from Office on Impeachment for, and Conviction of, Treason, Bribery, or other high Crimes and Misdemeanors.

Succession to the Presidency

U.S. CONSTITUTION, AMENDMENT XXV

Section 1. In case of the removal of the President from office or of his death or resignation, the Vice President shall become President.

Section 2. Whenever there is a vacancy in the office of the Vice President, the President shall nominate a Vice President who shall take office upon confirmation by a majority vote of both houses of Congress.

Section 3. Whenever the President transmits to the President pro tempore of the Senate and the Speaker of the House of Representatives his written declaration that he is unable to discharge the powers and duties of his office, and until he transmits to them a written declaration to the contrary, such powers and duties shall be discharged by the Vice President as Acting President.

Section 4. Whenever the Vice President and a majority of either the principal officers of the executive departments or of such other body as Congress may by law provide, transmit to the President pro tempore of the Senate and the Speaker of the House of Representatives their written declaration that the President is unable to discharge the powers and duties of his office, the Vice President shall immediately assume the powers and duties of the office as Acting President.

Thereafter, when the President transmits to the President pro tempore of the Senate and the Speaker of the House of Representatives his written declaration that no inability exists, he shall resume the powers and duties of his office unless the Vice President and a majority of either the principal officers of the executive department or of such other body as Congress may by law provide, transmit within four days to the President pro tempore of the Senate and the Speaker of the House of Representatives their written declaration that the President is unable to discharge the powers and duties of his office. Thereupon Congress shall decide the issue, assembling within forty-eight hours for that purpose if not in session. If the Congress, within twenty-one days after receipt of the latter written declaration, or, if Congress is not in session, within twenty-one days after Congress is required to assemble, determines by two-thirds vote of both houses that the President is unable to discharge the powers and duties of his office, the Vice-President shall continue to discharge the same as Acting President; otherwise, the President shall resume the powers and duties of his office. (Ratified in 1967)

President	*Died in*	*And was succeeded by Vice-President*
W. H. Harrison	1841	John Tyler
Zachary Taylor	1850	Millard Fillmore
Abraham Lincoln	1865	Andrew Johnson
James A. Garfield	1881	Chester A. Arthur
William McKinley	1901	Theodore Roosevelt
Warren G. Harding	1923	Calvin Coolidge
Franklin D. Roosevelt	1945	Harry S. Truman
John F. Kennedy	1963	Lyndon B. Johnson

	Resigned in	
Richard M. Nixon	1974	Gerald R. Ford

Presidential succession has never yet gone beyond the vice-presidency. By the Presidential Succession Act of 1947, as amended, the line of succession to the presidency, first to last, is:

Vice-President
Speaker of the House
President pro tempore of the Senate
Secretary of State
Secretary of the Treasury
Secretary of Defense

Attorney General
Secretary of the Interior
Secretary of Agriculture
Secretary of Commerce
Secretary of Labor
Secretary of Health and Human Services
Secretary of Housing and Urban Development
Secretary of Transportation
Secretary of Energy
Secretary of Education

Vacancies in the Vice-Presidency

The office of the vice-president has been vacant 18 times, for a total of more than 37 years.

Nine vice-presidents left the office vacant when they went to the White House to fill a presidential vacancy.

Seven vice-presidents died in office:

Vice-President	Died in	under President
George Clinton	1812	James Madison—1st term
Elbridge Gerry	1814	James Madison—2nd term
William R. King	1853	Franklin Pierce
Henry Wilson	1875	Ulysses S. Grant
Thomas A. Hendricks	1885	Grover Cleveland
Garret A. Hobart	1899	William McKinley
James S. Sherman	1912	William H. Taft

Two vice-presidents resigned: John C. Calhoun resigned in 1832 as vice-president under Andrew Jackson to become a U.S. senator. He had been vice-president since 1825, under both Jackson and John Quincy Adams. Spiro Agnew resigned in 1973 as vice-president under Nixon shortly before pleading "no contest" to charges of income tax evasion.

APPENDIX C

CONSTITUTIONAL AMENDMENTS EXPANDING THE SUFFRAGE

AMENDMENT XV

Section 1. The right of citizens of the United States to vote shall not be

denied or abridged by the United States or by any State on account of race, color, or previous condition of servitude. (Ratified in 1870)

AMENDMENT XVII
Section 1. The Senate of the United States shall be composed of two Senators from each State, elected by the people thereof, for six years; and each Senator shall have one vote. The electors in each State shall have the qualifications requisite for electors of the most numerous branch of the State Legislatures. (Ratified in 1913)

AMENDMENT XIX
Section 1. The right of citizens of the United States to vote shall not be denied or abridged by the United States or by any State on account of sex. (Ratified in 1920)

AMENDMENT XXIII
Section 1. The District constituting the seat of Government of the United States shall appoint in such manner as the Congress may direct:

A number of electors of President and Vice President equal to the whole number of Senators and Representatives in Congress to which the District would be entitled if it were a State, but in no event more than the least populous State; they shall be in addition to those appointed by the States, but they shall be considered, for the purposes of the election of President and Vice President, to be electors appointed by a State; and they shall meet in the District and perform such duties as provided by the twelfth article of amendment. (Ratified in 1961)

AMENDMENT XXIV
Section 1. The right of citizens of the United States to vote in any primary or other election for President or Vice President, for electors for President or Vice President, or for Senator or Representative in Congress, shall not be denied or abridged by the United States or any State by reason of failure to pay any poll tax or other tax. (Ratified in 1964)

AMENDMENT XXVI
Section 1. The right of citizens of the United States, who are eighteen years of age or older, to vote shall not be denied or abridged by the United States or by any State on account of age. (Ratified in 1971)

APPENDIX D

EVOLUTION OF THE
PRESIDENTIAL NOMINATION PROCESS

1789–1792   Early nonpartisan system. Washington twice elected unanimously with no formal nomination.

1796   Beginning of party control of political nominations generally and legislative caucus method of making presidential nominations. John Adams is last Federalist to be elected.

1800–1820   Federalist and Democratic-Republican (Jeffersonian) nominees, chosen in legislative caucus, battle regularly in elections.

1820–1824   "Era of Good Feeling." Monroe renominated by Democratic-Republicans by common consent with no formal action and wins in electoral college 231–1.

1824   Jackson defies legislative caucus and wins nomination of Tennessee legislature. Fails in election when presidential choice thrown into House of Representatives and John Quincy Adams wins in "corrupt bargain."

1828   Jackson is again nominated by Tennessee legislature and wins election, signaling new era by gaining power as result of well-organized popular movement. Caucus method of nomination now in disrepute.

1831   First national party convention in modern sense held in Baltimore by Anti-Masonic party. William Wirt nominated, but party fails to survive long.

1832   First Democratic national convention held in May in Baltimore as Jacksonian revolution continues. Jackson (for president) and Van Buren (for vice-president) nominated and elected.

1839   With convention method of nomination now becoming established, Whigs hold their first national convention. They elect two presidents but cannot survive the slavery turmoil.

1856   First Republican national convention held in June in

Philadelphia as new major party emerges. Frémont is first presidential candidate.

1860 Republicans nominate first winning presidential candidate in Abraham Lincoln.

1860–1908 Democratic and Republican national conventions dominate presidential nominations except for brief threat from Populists in 1890s.

1910 Oregon passes first presidential primary law as charges of bossism in conventions grow. Other states follow.

1912 First presidential election year with presidential primaries. New method allows Theodore Roosevelt to demonstrate popular support, but Taft wins nomination.

1972 Reforms in the Republican and Democratic parties.

1976 Thirty-one states held primaries.

1980 Thirty-five states held primaries.

APPENDIX E

ELECTORAL VOTES BY STATE

Total: 538   Needed to Win: 270

	1984	1980	CHANGE
California	47	45	+ 2
New York	36	41	− 5
Texas	29	26	+ 3
Pennsylvania	25	27	− 2
Illinois	24	26	− 2
Ohio	23	25	− 2
Florida	21	17	+ 4
Michigan	20	21	− 1
New Jersey	16	17	− 1
Massachusetts	13	14	− 1
North Carolina	13	13	
Georgia	12	12	
Indiana	12	13	− 1
Virginia	12	12	
Missouri	11	12	− 1

	1984	1980	CHANGE
Tennessee	11	10	+1
Wisconsin	11	11	
Louisiana	10	10	
Maryland	10	10	
Minnesota	10	10	
Washington	10	9	+1
Alabama	9	9	
Kentucky	9	9	
Colorado	8	7	+1
Connecticut	8	8	
Iowa	8	8	
Oklahoma	8	8	
South Carolina	8	8	
Arizona	7	6	+1
Kansas	7	7	
Mississippi	7	7	
Oregon	7	6	+1
Arkansas	6	6	
West Virginia	6	6	
Nebraska	5	5	
New Mexico	5	4	+1
Utah	5	4	+1
Hawaii	4	4	
Idaho	4	4	
Maine	4	4	
Montana	4	4	
Nevada	4	3	+1
New Hampshire	4	4	
Rhode Island	4	4	
Alaska	3	3	
Delaware	3	3	
District of Columbia	3	3	
North Dakota	3	3	
South Dakota	3	3	
Vermont	3	3	
Wyoming	3	3	

APPENDIX F

PROTECTION OF CANDIDATES FOR THE PRESIDENCY

The assassination of President William McKinley in 1901 provided the impetus for initiating Secret Service protection of presidents. But presidential aspirants were not given this security option until the assassination of Sen. Robert F. Kennedy 67 years later, when President Johnson issued an executive order calling for protection of all announced major candidates for the presidency. This later became law, with the provision that candidates could decline protection. In the 1976 campaign more than half a dozen candidates requested and received Secret Service protection.

A five-person advisory committee determines whether prospective candidates meet the criteria for protection. To qualify, a candidate must:

—be a declared candidate;
—have received financial contributions and be likely to qualify for federal matching funds; and
—conduct an active campaign.

There are, however, exceptions to these criteria. In 1979 Sen. Edward Kennedy was given Secret Service protection even though he had not formally declared his candidacy for president.

APPENDIX G

SIGNIFICANT PRESIDENTIAL ELECTIONS

With the electoral college system it is possible for a candidate to be elected by a majority of the electoral votes, even though he may not have had a majority of the popular votes throughout the nation (majority means one more than half).

Elected without popular majorities, but with popular pluralities (the most votes) in a field of more than two candidates:[3]

James K. Polk in 1844	Grover Cleveland in 1892
Zachary Taylor in 1848	Woodrow Wilson in 1912
James Buchanan in 1856	Woodrow Wilson in 1916
Abraham Lincoln in 1860	Harry S. Truman in 1948
James A. Garfield in 1880	John F. Kennedy in 1960
Grover Cleveland in 1884	Richard M. Nixon in 1968

Elected with neither majorities nor pluralities of *popular* votes:

John Quincy Adams in 1824 (election decided by House of Representatives)

Rutherford B. Hayes in 1876 (election decided by congressional electoral commission)

Benjamin Harrison in 1888 (received majority of *electoral* vote)

The closest presidential election in 76 years: In 1960 Kennedy's official plurality after recounts was 118,263 votes in a record 68 million-plus votes cast. His plurality percentage was the thinnest margin—less than one-half of 1 percent. Electoral votes cast were: 303 for Kennedy; 219 for Nixon; 15 for Sen. Harry F. Byrd of Virginia (from electors in Mississippi, Alabama, and Oklahoma). Kennedy won seven states (Delaware, Hawaii, Illinois, Minnesota, Missouri, New Jersey, New Mexico) by less than 1 percent of the popular vote in each.

These seven states had a total of 77 electoral votes—much more than enough to swing the election to him. Five additional states (Michigan, Nevada, Pennsylvania, South Carolina, Texas) gave Kennedy their electoral votes (87) with a less than 2 percent plurality of popular vote. Altogether these 12 states, in which Kennedy won with a less than 2 percent popular plurality, had a total electoral vote of 164, far more than half the electoral votes Kennedy received to win the election.

NOTES

Chapter 2

1. See V. O. Key, Jr., *Politics, Parties and Pressure Groups,* a classic work on American parties. Also see Frank J. Sorauf, *Party Politics in America.*

2. Realignment refers to lasting change in political behavior and party loyalties, generally in response to a stirring issue. Some political scientists believe there have been five major realignments in American political history. In 1800, the issue was the power of the national government; in 1828, Jacksonianism; in 1860, slavery; in 1896, monetary policy and capitalism; in 1932, the Depression. See Walter Dean Burnham, *Critical Elections and the Mainstream of American Politics.*

3. Key, *Politics, Parties and Pressure Groups,* p. 319.

4. For a historical perspective on the growth of third parties, see Daniel A. Mazmanian, *Third Parties in Presidential Elections.*

Chapter 3

1. Defined in the act as American Indians, Asian Americans (Chinese, Filipino, Japanese, Korean), Alaskan Natives or persons of Spanish heritage.

2. A number of studies include research on this subject and reach similar conclusions. Among the best known are *The American Voter* by Angus Campbell *et al.;* Lester W. Milbrath's *Political Participation; The Voter Decides* by Angus Campbell *et al.; Who Votes?* by Raymond Wolfinger and Steven Rosenstone; *Women and Politics* by Sandra Baxter and Marjorie Lansing; Gerald Pomper, *Voter's Choice;* V. O. Key, *The Responsible Electorate;* and Norman H. Nie, Sidney Verba and John R. Petrocik, *The Changing American Voter.*

3. David B. Hill and Norman R. Luttbeg, *Trends in American Electoral Behavior.*

4. Joint Center for Political Studies.

Chapter 4

1. The four books by Theodore H. White on the making of the president offer

some of the best material available on the preliminary period. Also, see White's *America in Search of Itself*.

2. See Walter Johnson, *How We Drafted Adlai Stevenson*.

3. For one study, see Edward W. Chester, *Radio, Television and American Politics*.

Chapter 5

1. Herbert Alexander, *Financing the 1980 Election*, p. 103.

2. The deduction was dropped in 1978, but the credit was retained.

3. A multicandidate committee must be registered with the FEC for six months, receive contributions from more than 50 persons and make contributions to five or more federal candidates.

4. An excellent history and analysis of PACs can be found in the Congressional Research Service publication by Joseph E. Cantor, *Political Action Committees: Their Evolution and Growth and Their Implications for the Political System*.

5. "Persons" can mean individuals or groups. All political committees also can contribute to party committees and to other political committees. Receipts and contributions must be disclosed to the FEC.

6. Alexander, *op. cit.*, p. 127.

7. *Ibid.*, p. 149.

8. Alexander, *op. cit.*, pp. 123 and 387.

9. *Ibid.*, pp. 318, 328, and Congressional Quarterly, *Dollar Politics*, pp. 82–83.

10. Congressional Quarterly, *op. cit.*, p. 93.

11. For discussion of these and other campaign issues, see Elizabeth Drew, *Politics and Money: The New Road to Corruption*.

Chapter 7

1. Judith N. Parris, *The Convention Problem*, p. 4.

2. The candidates operate by phone or through representatives. It has traditionally been considered bad form for candidates to appear at the convention hall before nominations are made.

Chapter 8

1. Richard Reeves, *A Ford, Not a Lincoln.*

Chapter 9

1. An "elector" is simply a person who elects someone else. The term *college* refers to a decision-making group such as the College of Cardinals, which elects the pope.

2. For comprehensive discussions of the development and operation of the electoral college system—its pros and cons and possible reforms—see League of Women Voters of the United States, *Who Should Elect the President?;* Joseph Gorman, *Elections: Electoral College Reform;* Lawrence D. Longley and Alan G. Brown, *The Politics of the Electoral College;* and Nelson W. Polsby and Aaron B. Wildavsky, *Presidential Elections.*

3. In 1876, the House decided which of two disputed sets of electoral votes to accept from certain southern states.

4. Before the adoption in 1933 of the Twentieth Amendment, presidents were inaugurated on March 4.

5. In an emergency, a president may take the oath of office before any official authorized to administer oaths, even a notary public. After the assassination of President John F. Kennedy in 1963, Lyndon Johnson was sworn in as president by Federal Judge Sarah Hughes in the presidential plane at the Dallas airport.

Appendix

1. By the Twentieth Amendment, adopted in 1933, the term of the president is to begin on January 20.

2. Under the Twentieth Amendment, Section 3, in case a president is not chosen before the time fixed for the beginning of his term, the vice-president elect shall act as president until a president shall have qualified.

3. Examples of third-party presidential nominees in this century who have received electoral votes: in 1912, Theodore Roosevelt, Progressive (Bull Moose) party—88 electoral votes; in 1924, Robert M. La Follette, Sr., Progressive—13 electoral votes; in 1948, J. Strom Thurmond, States' Rights party (Dixiecrat)—39 electoral votes; in 1968, George C. Wallace, American Independent party—46 electoral votes.

BIBLIOGRAPHY

Adamany, David W., and George E. Agree. *Political Money—A Strategy for Campaign Financing in America*. Baltimore: Johns Hopkins University Press, 1975.

Alexander, Herbert E. "Communications and Politics: The Media and the Message." *Law and Contemporary Problems*. Duke University School of Law, Durham, N.C., Spring 1971.

———. *Political Finance: Reform and Reality*. Philadelphia: American Academy of Political and Social Science, 1976.

———. *Financing the 1976 Election*. Washington, D.C.: Congressional Quarterly, Inc., 1979.

———. *Financing the 1980 Election*. Lexington, Mass.: Lexington Books, 1983.

"American Political Reform." *Current History*, August 1974.

Asher, Herbert B. *Presidential Elections and American Politics*. Homewood, Ill.: Dorsey Press, 1980.

Bach, Stanley, and George T. Sulzner. *Perspectives on the Presidency: A Collection*. Lexington, Mass.: D. C. Heath, 1974.

Barber, James D., ed. *Choosing the President*. Englewood Cliffs, N.J.: Prentice-Hall, 1974.

Barber, James David. *The Pulse of Politics*. New York: Norton, 1980.

Baxter, Sandra, and Marjorie Lansing. *Women and Politics: The Visible Majority*. Ann Arbor: University of Michigan Press, 1983.

Blackman, Paul H. *Presidential Primaries and the 1976 Elections*. Washington, D.C.: Heritage Foundation, 1975.

Blevens, Leon W. *The Young Voters Manual*. Totowa, N.J.: Littlefield, 1973.

Bode, Ken. "Black Democrats at the Tower of Babel." *New Republic*, December 27, 1975.

———. "Polls and Pols." *New Republic*, January 17, 1976.

Bone, Hugh. *American Politics and the Party System*. 4th ed. New York: McGraw-Hill, 1971.

Bruno, Jerry. *The Advance Man*. New York: Bantam Books, 1971.

Campbell, Angus et al. *The American Voter*. New York: John Wiley & Sons, 1960.

Cantor, Joseph E. *Political Action Committees: Their Evolution and Growth and Their Implications for the Political System*. Washington, D.C.: Congressional Research Service, Library of Congress, 1981; rev. ed., 1982.

Cantor, Robert D. *Voting Behavior and Presidential Elections*. Itasca, Ill.: F. E. Peacock, 1975.

Casey, Carol F. *Procedures for Selection of Delegates to the Democratic and Republican 1980 National Conventions: A Preliminary Survey of Applicable State Laws and Party Rules*. Congressional Research Service, Library of Congress, October 1979.

Chester, Edward W. *Radio, Television and American Politics*. New York: Sheed & Ward, 1969.

Civil Rights Commission. *Voting Rights Act—10 Years After*. Washington, D.C.: Government Printing Office, 1975.

Colburn, Kenneth S., and George A. Dalley. *The Congressional Black Caucus and Joint Center for Political Studies Guide to Participation in the Delegate Selection Process for the Democratic and Republican Party Conventions in 1976*. Washington, D.C.: Third National Institute for Black Elected Officials, 1975.

Crittenden, John A. *Parties and Elections in the United States*. Englewood Cliffs, N.J.: Prentice-Hall, 1982.

Crotty, William. *Party Reform*. New York: Longman, 1983.

Crouse, Timothy. *The Boys on the Bus: Riding with the Campaign Press Corps*. New York: Ballantine Books, 1974.

Davis, James W. *Presidential Primaries*. Westport, Conn.: Greenwood Press, 1980.

———. *Road to the White House*. Westport, Conn.: Greenwood Press, 1980.

Democratic National Committee. *Mandate for Reform*. Report of the Commission on Party Structure and Delegate Selection. Washington, D.C., 1970.
———. *Delegate Selection Rules for the 1976 Democratic National Convention*. Washington, D.C., 1975.
———. *Democrats All*. Report of the Commission on Delegate Selection and Party Structure. Washington, D.C., 1973.
DeVries, Walter, and V. Lance Tarrance. *Ticket Splitter: A New Force in American Politics*. Grand Rapids, Mich.: William B. Eerdmans, 1972.
Direct Popular Election of the President and Vice President of the United States. United States Congress, Senate Committee on the Judiciary, Subcommittee on the Constitution. Washington, D.C.: Government Printing Office, 1979.
Drew, Elizabeth. "Running." *New Yorker*, December 1, 1975.
———. *Portrait of an Election*. New York: Simon and Schuster, 1981.
———. *Politics and Money: The New Road to Corruption*. New York: Macmillan Publishing Co., Inc., 1983.
Dunn, Delmer D. *Financing Presidential Campaigns*. Washington, D.C.: Brookings Institution, 1972.
Durbin, Thomas M. *Nomination and Election of the President and Vice President of the United States*. Washington, D.C.: Government Printing Office, 1980.
Election of 1980, The. Chatham, N.J.: Chatham House, 1981.
"Election '84 Handbook: A Guide to the Candidates, the Issues and the Voters." *National Journal*, October 29, 1983.
Factual Campaign Information. Compiled under the direction of the Secretary of the Senate. Washington, D.C.: Government Printing Office, March 1976.
Flanigan, William H. *Political Behavior of the American Electorate*. Boston: Allyn & Bacon, 1968.
Germond, Jack. *Blue Smoke and Mirrors*. New York: Viking, 1981.
Githens, Marianne, and Jewel L. Prestage, eds. *A Portrait of Marginality: The Political Behavior of the American Woman*. New York: David McKay Co., Inc., 1977.
Gorman, Joseph. *Elections: Electoral College Reform*. Washington, D.C.: Congressional Research Service, Library of Congress, January 1976.
———. *Elections: Presidential Primaries*. Washington, D.C.: Congressional Research Service, Library of Congress, Issue Brief, continuously revised.
Hadley, Arthur T. *The Invisible Primary*. Englewood Cliffs, N.J.: Prentice-Hall, 1976.
Hess, Stephen. *The Presidential Campaign: The Leadership Selection Process After Watergate*. Washington, D.C.: Brookings Institution, 1974.
Hiebert, Ray E.; Robert F. Jones; John d'Arc Lorenze; and Ernest A. Lotito, eds. *The Political Image Merchants: Strategies for the Seventies*. Washington, D.C.: Acropolis Books, 1975.
Hill, David B., and Norman R. Luttbeg. *Trends in American Political Behavior*. 2nd ed. Itasca, Ill.: F. E. Peacock Publishers, 1983.
Hofstadter, Richard. *American Political Tradition*. New York: Random House, 1948.
Hoopes, Roy. "The Press and the Campaigns: Back on the Bus in '76." *Democratic Review*, October/November 1975.
Humphrey, Hubert H. "How the President Can Help Improve Vice-Presidential Selection." *Congressional Record*, vol. 119, no. 202, December 21, 1973.
Johnson, Walter. *How We Drafted Adlai Stevenson*. New York: Alfred A. Knopf, 1955.
Keech, William, and Donald Matthews. *The Party's Choice*. Washington, D.C.: Brookings Institution, 1976.
Kelley, Stanley. *Interpreting Elections*. Princeton, N.J.: Princeton University Press, 1983.
Kerr, Virginia. "The ABCs of Delegate Selection." *Ms.*, January 1976.
Kessel, John Howard, *Presidential Campaign Politics*. Homewood, Ill.: Dorsey Press, 1980.
Key, V. O., Jr. *Politics, Parties and Pressure Groups*, 5th ed. New York: Thomas Y. Crowell, 1964.
Lang, Kurt, and Gladys Engel Lang. *Voting and Non-Voting: Implications of Broadcasting Returns Before Polls Are Closed*. Waltham, Mass.: Blaisdell, 1968.
League of Women Voters Education Fund. *Election '76: Issues Not Images*. Washington, D.C., 1976.

League of Women Voters of the United States. *Who Should Elect the President?* Washington, D.C., 1969.

Longley, Lawrence D., and Alan G. Braun. *The Politics of the Electoral College.* New Haven: Yale University Press, 1972.

MacNeil, Robert. *The People Machine: The Influence of Television on American Politics.* New York: Harper & Row, 1968.

Malbin, Michael. "Political Report/Party System Approaching Crossroads in 1976 Election." *National Journal,* May 31, 1975.

———. "Political Report/New Campaign Finance Law Faces Legal, Political Tests." *National Journal,* July 12, 1975.

———. "Political Report/Democratic Delegate Rules Influencing Candidates' Strategies." *National Journal,* December 6, 1975.

Mandel, Ruth B. *In the Running: The New Woman Candidate.* New Haven: Ticknor & Fields, 1981.

Matthews, Donald. *Perspectives on Presidential Selection.* Washington, D.C.: Brookings Institution, 1973.

May, Ernest R., and Janet Fraser. *Campaign, '72.* Cambridge, Mass.: Harvard University Press, 1973.

Mazmanian, Daniel A. *Third Parties in Presidential Elections: Studies in Presidential Selection.* Washington, D.C.: Brookings Institution, 1974.

McGinniss, Joe. *The Selling of the President 1968.* New York: Trident, 1969.

Miles, William. *The Image Makers.* Metuchen, N.J.: Scarecrow Press, 1979.

Minow, Newton N.; John B. Martin; and Lee M. Mitchell. *Presidential Television.* Twentieth Century Fund Report. New York: Basic Books, 1973.

Nomination and Election of the President and Vice President of the United States. Compiled under the direction of the Secretary of the Senate. Washington, D.C.: Government Printing Office, March 1976.

Parris, Judith N. *The Convention Problem: Issues in Reform of Presidential Nominating Procedures.* Washington, D.C.: Brookings Institution, 1972.

Parris, Judith N., and Richard Baine. *Convention Decisions and Voting Records.* Washington, D.C.: Brookings Institution, 1973.

Patterson, Thomas E. *The Mass Media Election.* New York: Praeger, 1980.

Peirce, Neal R., and Lawrence D. Longley. *The People's President.* Rev. ed. New Haven: Yale University Press, 1981.

Perry, James M. *The New Politics: The Expanding Technology of Political Manipulation.* New York: Clarkson N. Potter, 1968.

———. *Us and Them: How the Press Covered the 1972 Elections.* New York: Clarkson N. Potter, 1972.

Petersen, Svend. *A Statistical History of the American Presidential Elections.* Westport, Conn.: Greenwood Press, 1981.

Phillips, Kevin P. *The Emerging Republican Majority.* Garden City, N.Y.: Doubleday, 1970.

———. *Mediacracy: American Parties and Politics in the Communications Age.* Garden City, N.Y.: Doubleday, 1975.

Polsby, Nelson W. *Presidential Elections.* New York: Scribner, 1980.

Polsby, Nelson W., and Aaron Wildavsky. *Presidential Elections: Strategies of American Electoral Politics.* 4th ed. New York: Charles Scribner's Sons, 1976.

Pomper, Gerald. *Voters' Choice: Varieties of American Electoral Behavior.* New York: Harper & Row, 1975.

Presidential Elections since 1789. 3rd ed. Washington, D.C.: Congressional Quarterly, Inc., 1983.

Ranney, Austin. *Curing the Mischiefs of Faction: Party Reform in America.* Berkeley: University of California Press, 1975.

Reeves, Richard. *A Ford, Not a Lincoln: The Decline of American Leadership.* New York: Harcourt Brace Jovanovich, 1975.

Republican National Committee. *Report of the Rule 29 Committee.* Washington, D.C., 1975.

Ripon Society and Clifford W. Brown, Jr. *Jaws of Victory.* Boston: Little, Brown, 1974.

Roper, Burns W. "Distorting the Voice of the People." *Columbia Journalism Review,* November/December 1975.

Roseboom, Eugene Holloway, and Alfred E. Eckes, Jr. *A History of Presidential Elections: From George Washington to Jimmy Carter*. New York: Macmillan, 1979.

Rosenstone, Steven J. *Forecasting Presidential Elections*. New Haven: Yale University Press, 1983.

Rubin, Richard L. *Press, Party and Presidency*. New York: Norton, 1981.

Scammon, Richard M. *America Votes*. America Votes Series, vol. 10. Washington, D.C.: Congressional Quarterly, Inc., continuously revised.

Scammon, Richard M., and Ben J. Wattenberg. *The Real Majority*. New York: Coward-McCann, 1971.

Schwartzman, Edward. *Campaign Craftsmanship: A Professional Guide to Campaigning for Elective Office*. New York: Universe Books, 1973.

Shadegg, Stephen C. *How to Win an Election*. New York: Taplinger, 1964.

Smith, Jeffrey A. *American Presidential Elections*. New York: Praeger, 1980.

Sundquist, James L. *Dynamics of the Party System: Alignment and Realignment of Political Parties in the United States*. rev. ed. Washington, D.C.: Brookings Institution, 1983.

Television Coverage of the 1980 Elections. Norwood, N.J.: Ablex Publishing Corp., 1983.

Thompson, Hunter S. *Fear and Loathing: On the Campaign Trail '72*. New York: Popular Library, 1973.

United Steel Workers of America with the cooperation of Kramer Associates. *Senior Power: A Political Action Handbook for Senior Citizens*. Washington, D.C., 1974.

Wayne, Stephen J. *The Road to the White House*. New York: St. Martin's Press, 1983.

White, Theodore H. *The Making of the President 1960*. New York: Atheneum, 1961.

————. *The Making of the President 1964*. New York: Atheneum, 1965.

————. *The Making of the President 1968*. New York: Atheneum, 1969.

————. *The Making of the President 1972*. New York: Atheneum, 1973.

————. *America in Search of Itself*. New York: Harper & Row, 1982.

Wilson, James Q. *The 1980 Election*. Lexington, Mass.: D. C. Heath, 1981.

Wolfinger, Raymond E., and Steven J. Rosenstone, *Who Votes?* New Haven: Yale University Press, 1980.

Wyckoff, Gene. *The Image Candidates: American Politics in the Age of Television*. New York: Macmillan, 1968.

INDEX